"I still believe that standing up for the truth of God is the greatest thing in the world. This is the end of life."

Martin Luther King, Jr.,
"The Most Durable Power"

Robert R. Hann

• THE LYMAN BEECHER LECTURES IN PREACHING •

The End of Words

The Language of Reconciliation in a Culture of Violence

RICHARD LISCHER

William B. Eerdmans Publishing Company

Grand Rapids, Michigan / Cambridge, U.K.

Published 2005 by

Wm. B. Eerdmans Publishing Co.

2140 Oak Industrial Drive N.E., Grand Rapids, Michigan 49505 /
P.O. Box 163, Cambridge CB3 9PU U.K.

Paperback edition 2008

Printed in the United States of America

18 17 16 15   10 9 8 7 6

Library of Congress Cataloging-in-Publication Data

Lischer, Richard.

The end of words: the language of reconciliation
in a culture of violence / Richard Lischer.

p.   cm.   — (The Lyman Beecher lectures in preaching)

Includes bibliographical references.

ISBN 978-0-8028-6280-8 (pbk.: alk. paper)

1. Preaching.

2. Reconciliation — Religious aspects — Christianity.
I. Title.   II. Lyman Beecher lectures.

BV4211.3.L57   2005
251 — dc22

2005040109

www.eerdmans.com

Contents

vii

Preface

The end is where we start from.

T. S. Eliot, *Four Quartets*

These chapters on preaching appear in an era when "everything has changed." In the context of worldwide terrorism, war, and religious conflict, how is it possible to speak or hear the message of Jesus Christ? Does the proclamation of his peace have a chance amidst the clamorous language of violence? In New York City the authorities have banned public speeches in official commemorations of the attack. It seems words will no longer do on such an occasion.

Has everything really changed, or have the vocation of the preacher and the ministry of reconciliation merely been given a terrible new urgency?

When Jesus began his ministry of preaching, he did so using the language of the end of history. In the synagogue at Nazareth, he announced to his neighbors that the Day of the Lord's deliverance was in the process of dawning in the words of his sermon. It seemed preposterous at the time, but since that day in Nazareth every preacher anointed with his Spirit has spoken from the perspective of the end. Even those who preach in circumstances as ordinary as the local church or mission chapel are imbued with extraordinary eschatological reach. Sermons no longer talk about the end, they are signs and emblems of it.

Preachers continue to follow Jesus' example but in a culture that is suffering a certain exhaustion with words. Mass violence overrides the significance of language. The centralization of the means of communication only ensures that everyone thinks and talks roughly the same. The first casualty of the information age is truth. Passion and beauty have become expendable virtues.

But the poet says, "The end is where we start from," and that is true for preachers as well. In the following chapters I will trace a path from some of the frustrations and dead ends of language through the nurturing tasks of reading the Scripture and re-narrating the story, to the true and eternal end of language itself: the message of reconciliation. In an era when "everything has changed" politically and culturally, the true prophets will be those who overcome "the rhetoric of the barricades," as Shaw called it, and speak the word of God's peace.

I first gave these chapters orally as the Lyman Beecher Lectures at Yale University. I shall always be grateful to

Richard Wood, David Bartlett, and the faculty of Yale Divinity School for inviting me to participate in this great tradition.

Chapter Two was originally delivered as a part of the Macleod Lectures on Preaching at Princeton Theological Seminary, where my hosts Thomas Gillespie and David Bartow offered their generous hospitality.

Portions of these chapters were also given as the Yost Lectures at Lutheran Southern Seminary and the Gray Lectures at Duke Divinity School. At Duke, Greg Jones gave the manuscript a careful reading, and I have greatly benefited from his suggestions.

I have expanded and enriched the material of the spoken word to make these lectures accessible to a reading audience. The trick was to do so without sacrificing my own speaking voice in the process. I hope I have succeeded.

This book is dedicated to my son Adam, who along with my wife made the trip to Yale and listened to these chapters in their original form. His love and support have meant more to me than I can express.

VOCATION

Chapter One

The Ultimate Vocation

In 1919 William Butler Yeats composed both the preface and the postscript to the twentieth century. With a prophet's instinct for catastrophe, he heralded the changing of the guard from one age and one construction of reality to another. His poem was called "The Second Coming," and it begins like this:

> Turning and turning in the widening gyre
> The falcon cannot hear the falconer;
> Things fall apart; the centre cannot hold;
> Mere anarchy is loosed upon the world,
> The blood-dimmed tide is loosed, and everywhere
> The ceremony of innocence is drowned;
> The best lack all conviction, while the worst
> Are full of passionate intensity.

According to the poet, the crisis of the modern world is a crisis of speaking and hearing, of call and response. A creation that was once on intimate listening terms with its creator now spins out of control. He tells of a falconer who can no longer communicate with his falcon because the creature, whose orbits have grown increasingly erratic, cannot hear the commands of the one who trained it. Its mission has descended into mere anarchy — "mere" because, when compared to its original responsiveness to its master, the bird's flight is little more than a chaotic scramble to freedom.

Whatever it was the poet believed binds life to life in a spiritual coherence was no longer working. He was doubtless thinking of the Great War, the Bolshevik Revolution, anarchism on the continent, and the troubles in his beloved Ireland. He had not even glimpsed with his physical eyes the terrors of our own day, when even a powerful country like the United States would come to feel like "a closed and guarded palace in a city gripped by the plague."[1]

Why begin with Yeats? Because if his fellow poet Ezra Pound was right when he claimed that poets are the antennae of the race, Yeats had his antennae out early. He is our first alert. He sounds the first modern alarm that whoever has a serious vocation in language and proposes to communicate from depth to depth will be in trouble. Even preachers will say their "Thus says the Lords" in dis-

---

1. The phrase is Conor Cruise O'Brien's in his comments on "The Second Coming" in *On the Eve of the Millennium* (New York: Free Press, 1994), p. 132. For the complete text of the poem see *The Poems of W. B. Yeats*, ed. Richard Finneran (New York: MacMillan, 1989).

integrating circumstances. Even they will speak against the grain of their environment among people with a diminished capacity to hear.

The Silence of the Words

The multiple traumas of the twentieth and now the twenty-first centuries have produced a sense of futility among those with a vocation in language. Violence has a way of making a mockery of words. After Auschwitz, Hiroshima, Vietnam, Cambodia, Rwanda, all the words sound hollow. What does one *say* after a televised beheading? The proclamation of God's justice or God's love meets a wall of resistance first in the throat of the proclaimer, then in the ears of the hearer.

When true convictions give way to bigger and bigger lies told with increasingly "passionate intensity," the poet knows that it is time to keep silence. Later in the century, certain theologians and preachers would join the poets in denouncing the corruption of language. When the message of Jesus Christ can be Nazified or made the tool of racism, anti-Semitism, apartheid, or capitalism, it is time for preachers to shut up and take stock of themselves.

Before any prophet speaks, the prophet is absolutely positive that he or she must *not* speak. Moses claimed a speech impediment; Isaiah confessed his own impurity;

Jeremiah appealed to his inexperience. After the temple was destroyed, the prophet Ezekiel was transported to a refugee camp at Tel Abib. There he sat for seven days stupefied among the refugees, or, as one translation has it, "in a catatonic state." Imagine the denizens of the twentieth century, beginning with the ninety-three million dead in wars, gazing up from their mass graves or through the barbed wire of their camps, stupefied, catatonic. Something has ended. Visit the Holocaust Museum or Dachau. The normative demeanor is silence.

How ironic that poets and preachers, whose stock and trade is words and nothing else, should respond to tragedy with a call to silence, that they, of all people, should feel that the human race has come to the end of words.

No prophet questioned the feasibility of the word more searchingly than the prisoner Dietrich Bonhoeffer, who wrote from his cell in April 1944, "The time when people could be told everything by means of words, whether theological or pious, is over."[2] He said the world had come of age, by which he meant that men and women have outgrown the set of symbols from which they once received ultimate meaning. It has become possible to pursue science, art, ethics, and even religion

2. Dietrich Bonhoeffer, *Letters and Papers from Prison*, trans. Reginald Fuller, Frank Clark, et al., ed. Eberhard Bethge (New York: Simon and Schuster, 1997 [1953]), p. 279; cf. 329, 360.

apart from reliance on God or the comforts of religious language.

Bonhoeffer would have defined religion as any recourse to the transcendent that enables human beings to avoid the claims of Jesus Christ. In that view, religion has nothing to offer those who follow Jesus. Of what use is pious language that distracts believers from the concrete duties of discipleship? Any word that can breathe on its own apart from the life of the community is by definition false. For, according to Bonhoeffer, Jesus is already so materially present in the world that he and his followers have nothing to gain from the rules and rhetoric of religion. Nor should the preacher try to build on the assured results of science, politics, or philosophy, for these are no longer foundations for something else but free-standing idols in their own right. If there is to be preaching, all it can do is conform itself to the life of Christ in the community. Christians may practice their faith by maintaining a "hidden discipline" of prayer and love, but Bonhoeffer foresaw a wall rising between the pulpit and an audience that had outgrown it.

Christianity in America has followed a different course than the one Bonhoeffer predicted, but his basic assertion informs the thesis of this and succeeding chapters. The preacher's job is at once easier and more impossible than many have imagined, for he or she is trying to do nothing less than shape the language of the sermon to a living reality among the people of God — to make it conform to Jesus. The sermon, in fact, *is* Jesus trying to speak once again in his own community, but because he has assumed the full extent of our fallibility, the power of his word is hidden and often disregarded by the world. Nevertheless, believers continue to organize their common life of mission, worship, and service around the presence of Christ in their midst. The preacher does the same for speech, as he or she models for the community a distinctively Christlike way of speaking in an uncomprehending and often hostile world.

The theologian Bonhoeffer understood that preaching has become hard not merely as a result of extrinsic developments, such as the rise of modern science or the threats of dictators. Preaching bears the impossible weight of its own message, which is God's willingness to be pushed out of the world and onto a cross. Preaching has to conjure with its own apparent irrelevance. God (and the preacher) can relate to the world only via the great symbol of marginalization, the cross, and by means of the hidden presence of God's chosen instrument, the marginalized Man for Others. Paradoxically, God can communicate with us only by means of the one who remained silent before his accusers, whose death was so irrelevant that it was not even recorded by the authorities. Bonhoeffer understood better than any of his generation the incongruity of standing on a soapbox, puffing out your chest, and making a speech about the crucified God.

We find Bonhoeffer's theology a little intense for our

tastes. His world of concentration camps and air raids seems far removed from our current revival of spirituality. Contemporary religion focuses on its own successes and avoids at all costs the paradox of the cross, a move that has produced a flood of compensatory words. There is an irrepressible chattiness about our religion, one that was utterly foreign to Bonhoeffer and those of his generation who were living just beyond their means on the boundaries of church and religious language.

Bonhoeffer ruefully tells the story of a terrible air raid during which one of his fellow prisoners cried out to God for help. He recalls that in this opportunity to witness all he could do was assure the man that the bombing would be over soon and not to worry. "Those who had been bombed out came to me the next morning for a bit of comfort. But I'm afraid I'm bad at comforting; I can listen all right, but I can hardly ever find anything to say."[3]

Why is it that when we enter life's deep places — a friend's betrayal, a challenging or dangerous job, the death of a child — we so often feel at a loss for words or prefer to let our actions do the talking? When the occasion demands a spoken word of forgiveness, judgment, or hope, why are these words so hard to come by?

Those who are preachers have paced about an empty room or stood in a deserted chancel on a Saturday night, hoping that some word will be given. We were not

3. Bonhoeffer, *Letters and Papers*, pp. 199, 203.

9

warned about this particular problem. The New Testament contains an implicit theology of preaching but no operating instructions or tips for effective speaking. The closest Paul comes to rhetorical strategy is in the Corinthian correspondence, where he promises that he will not adapt his gospel to prevailing standards of communication, but defy them. What Paul offers is a mystical homiletic by which the word of Christ's death and resurrection is properly spoken only by one who is materially embedded in all the dying and rising that occurs on a daily basis in ministry. It goes without saying in the New Testament that such speaking will be occasionally dangerous and always accompanied by suffering, but never difficult. We never meet an apostle pacing around the catacombs on Saturday night trying to think of something to say.

It is not for lack of resources that the sermon comes hard. Some who teach preaching occasionally imply that if you do your exegesis carefully and trust your theological training, the sermon will preach itself. But . . . the exegesis has been completed since Wednesday. The preacher's theology is impeccable. The *New York Times* has been consulted. Homiletics websites have been visited. And yet, the wordsmith is fresh out of words. Not, I repeat, for lack of biblical information or fetching illustrations, but because the path to authentic expression has closed. Yes, Bonhoeffer's world is far from ours, but his experience of the end of words survives as a familiar moment in the weekly ritual of sermon preparation.

A Sea of Words

Not fifty years before Bonhoeffer wrote his letters, G. K. Chesterton created an unforgettable Victorian image of Christian dogma as a great spike that fits exactly into a vast emptiness in the world with the result, said Chesterton, that "once these two parts of the two machines had come together . . . all the other parts fitted and fell in with an eerie exactitude." He continues, "I could hear bolt after bolt over all the machinery falling into place with a kind of click of relief" — an image ("click") C. S. Lewis would repeat in describing the harmonious aftermath of his own conversion.[4] It is a nice industrial image, but one that has gone the way of pipes, fittings, and the industrial age itself. It is precisely that "click of relief," signaling the perfect fit between revelation and its receptors, that Bonhoeffer and his successors could not hear.

Indeed, contemporary preachers cannot help but notice a growing dissonance between message and sensorium, between the gospel and the all-encompassing sea

4. Gilbert K. Chesterton, *Orthodoxy* (New York: Doubleday, 1990 [1908]), p. 79. C. S. Lewis, *Surprised by Joy* (New York: Harcourt Brace, 1955), p. 222.

of words, images, and ideologies within which we attempt to communicate it. Hence the rising urgency, even desperation, on the part of preachers to find just the right frequency for their message. The hymnodist might have been speaking for the besieged preacher when he asked, "What language shall I borrow/to thank thee dearest friend?" Some ministers have turned to the didactic or teaching sermon, in the conviction that ours is the most biblically tone-deaf generation ever. Others have given up on the sermon in its traditional form and replaced it with informal group discussions in a Starbucks-setting or film clips from *The Lord of the Rings* in hopes that the service might build on cultural resonances.

What language shall I borrow? An odd question when you stop to think, and one with a long and controversial history. Over the years, preachers have not been satisfied to speak from the embedded position. They have not been content with the starkness of the New Testament's theology of the word. They have sought other languages with which to communicate the gospel. When I was a seminarian, we all preached "existentially" after the manner of Bultmann, in the confidence that the existentialist analysis of the human predicament was pretty much the same as Paul's. When we weren't preaching existentially, we donned our white coats, lit our pipes, and preached therapeutically, in the equally misplaced confidence that psychologist Carl Rogers's view of the person was not all that different from Jesus'.

As exciting as those dialogues were, that is not where the action is today. Between religion and philosophy or Christianity and psychology you can draw a line and decide to cross it or not. In our current situation of total information, however, the lines are blurred. The preacher does not contend with competing messages that are easily named but with principalities and powers that envelop us and swim effortlessly beside us in the sea of words. The average American is subjected to approximately six thousand messages per day. Why should one of them called "gospel" stand out? What is one little message among so many?

Most of us like to think we have adapted to the information technology that surrounds us and harnessed it to the needs of the kingdom, but those who are preachers know the true and lively word — so rich in paradox, metaphor, and narrative, so demanding of community and time for absorption — does not match up well with its digitalized environment.

too true

Our new electronic nervous system promises what the philosopher Jean-François Lyotard calls "[p]erfect information at any given moment."[5] And when you think

5. Jean-François Lyotard, *The Postmodern Condition: A Report on Knowledge,* trans. Geoff Bennington and Brian Massumi (Minneapolis: University of Minnesota Press, 1984 [1979]), p. 67. Lyotard writes, "The nature of knowledge cannot survive unchanged within this context of general transformation. It can fit into the new channels, and become operational, only if learning is translated into quantities of

13

about it, that's exactly what we all expect. When we get home after a hard day at the office, we want to open a cold drink, put our feet up, tune in or dial up, and watch a war or a hurricane or some other crisis as it unfolds in real time. Lyotard also claims that any knowledge that does not mutate and adapt to the available technology in order to be bought and sold as information, cannot survive. If he is right, he is publishing the sermon's obituary, for there will be no such thing as communicating for the sake of the sheer goodness of the thing communicated, which is the very genius and freedom of the pulpit.

Our sensorium positions hi-tech versions of Ezekiel's wheels within wheels, their rims bulging with electronic eyes. As they silently encircle and monitor the planet, they give a synoptic account of all that is real and true. They transmit a quantity of information that would have staggered the imagination of Galileo or Erasmus. No single perspective is sufficiently compelling to integrate the many facts, stories, and images made available to us. No single narrative can provide a deep enough basket for the fragments of our lives. Instead, the catholicity of the medium itself exercises an authority greater than any one of its constitutive messages. We have become bit players in

_____

information. We can predict that anything in the constituted body of knowledge that is not translatable in this way will be abandoned and that the direction of new research will be dictated by the possibility of its eventual results being translatable into computer language" (p. 4).

a pageant too big to be comprehended by any of us. These may be "the days of miracle and wonder" the poet sings about, but the miracle does not come from the transcendent God but from the new transcendence made possible by electronic awareness of one another. It is not that we are made in the image of God that makes us so wonderful, but that our images can be comprehended in the eye of the universal camera.

The totality of the structure contains an infinite supply of choices, and they are free. All subjectivities are permissible within the domain of this new objectivity. We are free to select what works for us, what pleases us, or what interferes least with our lifestyle. Within this totality any expression of faith is appropriate and any religion true so long as it does not question the priority of the system or the individual's right to choose from its rich menu of options. All that is necessary to our well-being is controlled by a few enlightened conglomerates that own the wires connecting us to one another, and by our government, which guarantees our right to personal opinion and its free expression. As it is written above the main portal of the CIA headquarters, "Ye shall know the truth, and the truth shall make you free."

It is a truism that whoever controls the vast apparatuses of discourse in a society controls the society as well. On most controversial issues, the actual words Americans hear in the media are blandly amoral and nontheological. It is as if we were all living our lives, raising our kids, and making our laws beneath an empty sky in a god-less universe. For example, over the past three administrations, the United States has either been at war or threatening war with Iraq. During this period we have learned more from media analysts about strategic weaponry and military tactics than we can possibly absorb. But morally, we have learned nothing. We know what we *can* do but are ignorant of what we *ought* to do. We don't even have a language for discussing our ignorance.

Occasionally, politicians claim God's blessing upon selected wars, but the word "God" functions only as a cipher for the national interest. When God is mentioned at all, it is not a god we know. It is not the Trinitarian God whose interior relationships are guided by love between Father, Son, and Spirit, but rather the god of war, who does not relate to anyone but only dictates. We hear no serious voices in the conglomerate-controlled media raising moral let alone theological questions about war. No CNN analyst dares to measure war against the will of a Higher Being in whom the vast majority of the viewership professes to believe. No one so much as mentions issues that appear on every other page of the Old Testament, questions of idolatry, violence, and the suffering of innocents. As Martin Luther King said about another war long ago, "We have allowed our technology to outrun our theology." Our sensorium has reduced the kerygma, which originated in the public execution of the Son of God, to personal opinion in the ghetto of religious programming.

16

And many religious groups are thriving in the ghetto. According to Stanley Hauerwas, the mainline churches have tacitly agreed to "police themselves" by eliminating the radical claims of Jesus and his kingdom from their public vocabulary.[6] They have accommodated their rhetoric to the bloodless cadences of civil discourse, a discourse that deftly equates *normative* with *secular*. The churches have preached the virtues of tolerance, privacy, freedom, and equal rights — to say nothing of war and dominion — without explicitly subjecting these norms to the claims of Jesus Christ and the kingdom of God, with the result that many American churchgoers have come to assume that the "we" in most sermons refers not to the church but to the nation.

Preachers are always trying to carve out a special sphere of influence for the word of God. They try to protect the Bible from politics or science by celebrating its unique properties as divine revelation and by restricting its applicability to personal and cultic activities. With significant variations, this tendency to disembody the word has been the strategy of Protestant scholastics, fundamentalists, and adherents of the Biblical Theology movement, each of whom has attempted to demonstrate how the special characteristics of the word of God guarantee its authority and effectiveness.

6. Stanley Hauerwas, *Dispatches from the Front* (Durham, N.C.: Duke University Press, 1994), p. 93.

But every formal claim we make for the word, our culture absorbs, affirms, and trumps. The word is personal, even intimate, but it cannot compete with television's uncanny knack for simulating intimacy. Viewers "know" their favorite talk-show hosts better than they know their preacher. Capitalism works by infusing personal values into an impersonal system of consumption: "We don't build computers; we build relationships," says one advertisement.

The word of God is brimming with vivid images, but they pale beside the creations of Madison Avenue. The Bible's stories are "fraught with background," as the literary critic Erich Auerbach insisted. They can be understood only against the backdrop of Israel's long and dramatic history with God. Cultural images, on the other hand, glimmer on the surface of things and require no story and no training or preparation.

The word of God claims to effect change, even transformation, in the hearer's life, but the forces of marketing accomplish the same with persuasive skills unimagined by the preacher. "Yes," we counter, "but our message has a content, that of death and resurrection"; but before the words are out of our mouth we meet them on bumper stickers, Powerpoints, and in the clichés of motivational speakers.

What I have represented as a sea of words the prophet Ezekiel characterized as a national cemetery. Our setting is marked by white noise, his by white bones and the stillness of death. Ezekiel was called to prophesy deliverance from Israel's tomb. The word of the Lord still comes to the preacher and says, "Prophesy, mortal one, prophesy to the bones." But first the mortal one must recognize the deadly seriousness of the task. For the very language that informs his message is undergoing a kind of death and re-figuration. Every week the preacher must begin from the end of words.

The Retreat from the Word

About halfway through each semester of the introductory preaching class a few concerned students drop by my office individually or take me aside in the hall to tell me something they suspect I do not know. "Preaching is hard," they say.

"Really?" I reply. "You find these assignments difficult? Not the cushion against Church History and Theology you were counting on?"

"It's not that," they say. "It's just that — it's hard," by which they mean, Important.

"Does it get any easier?" they ask, "this business of coming up with a sermon?"

"Oh yes," I assure them pastorally, "much easier. Once you learn to follow the proper schemes and steps I am teaching you in this course. It's all a matter of method."

But even as I reassure them, I hear the voices of

preachers of every age saying, "You lie. You know it *never* gets easier!" I hear the complaints of those who have found the spoken word to be an intolerably heavy burden. I hear old Martin Luther, fed up with Wittenberg and Wittenbergers, complain, "I would rather carry stones than preach one sermon." I hear poor John Bunyan confessing that he sometimes feels like shouting obscenities at his congregation! I hear young Reinhold Niebuhr worrying to his diary that if he doesn't get his act together the weekly sermon will become "a terrible chore." I hear a tired Martin Luther King Jr. describe "the calling to speak" as a "vocation of agony."[7] And bear in mind that King is not alluding to the dangers of civil rights leadership or his own personal discouragement. He refers to the responsibility of preaching, the tyranny of words over the one who is called to utter them.

In the matter of the preacher's discontent, art has imitated life. In all American literature, you would be hard-pressed to find one happy, well-adjusted preacher.

---

7. Martin Luther King Jr., "Why I Am Opposed to the War in Vietnam" (April 30, 1967), quoted in Richard Lischer, *The Preacher King* (New York: Oxford, 1995), p. 187. On weariness with preaching, see *Luther's Works,* 51, *Sermons* I, ed. and trans. John W. Doberstein (Philadelphia: Fortress, 1959): "I would rather be stretched upon a wheel or carry stones than preach one sermon" (p. 222). See also John Bunyan, *Grace Abounding* (New York: Oxford, 1998), p. 82; Reinhold Niebuhr, *Leaves from the Notebook of a Tamed Cynic* (Louisville: Westminster/John Knox, 1980 [1927]), p. 12.

Whether Arthur Dimsdale in Hawthorne's *The Scarlet Letter* or Gabriel Grimes in James Baldwin's *Go Tell It on the Mountain,* the preacher is forever suspended between the holiness of the message and the shame of his own unworthiness. When Faulkner said, "The only thing worth writing about is the human heart in conflict with itself," he could have been talking about preachers.

In Flannery O'Connor's *Wise Blood* we meet Hazel Motes, a preacher who does not want to be a preacher but is captivated by his awful calling. He has a shiny blue preacher suit, a black tie, and a spiffy flat hat, which identify him as a preacher sure-enough. When he says to his taxi-driver, "I ain't any preacher," the cabbie doesn't buy it. So Haze adds, "I don't believe in anything." As he hastily departs the taxi the driver calls after him, "That's the trouble with you preachers. . . . You've all got too good to believe in anything."[8]

Perhaps we can't identify with these extreme reactions. Perhaps our feelings about preaching lie closer to ambivalence than agony. Ambivalence means you want to do something, *and* you do not want to do it. Both. It means there is nothing you desire more than to speak for the Lord, *and* there is nothing you despise more than the risk involved in doing so. Ambivalence means you believe in the power of God's word, *and* you haven't seen it lately

---

8. Flannery O'Connor, *Wise Blood,* in *Three by Flannery O'Connor* (New York: Signet, n.d. [1947]), pp. 21-22.

in your ministry. It means you live by the nourishment of the word, *and* you are a very busy professional.

Most ministers were "set apart for the gospel," as Paul says of himself at the beginning of Romans, by means of the spoken word with a view to the ministry of the word. The preacher's vocation was once a kind of circle that began and ended in the word. Whatever it was that made you a minister was aimed at its eventual public expression. The minister's whole existence was concentrated to a point of declaration.[9] Today, however, the circle has been broken.

Our culture devalues proclamation while elevating other associated forms of ministry such as counseling or community work. As a matter of public policy, the wider culture still wants something like ministry, much as it encourages charity and volunteerism, but it thinks it can have it without the word of God. Faith-based initiatives are fine so long as no preaching is attached.

Protestant ministers compliantly disempowered themselves by creating substitutes for the authority of the word of God. Ministers who were threatened by the professionalism of the doctors and lawyers distanced themselves from the parochialism of the word: The pastoral-care people invented medical-sounding credentials for their members. Military chaplains demanded

9. The phrase is Joseph Sittler's in *The Anguish of Preaching* (Philadelphia: Fortress, 1966), p. 8.

officer-rank in the armed forces. Seminary professors acquired Ph.D. degrees from secular universities. Parish pastors discovered the D.Min. to be a useful credential. We call our divinity graduates *magister,* master, which is a far cry from *diakonos* or *doulos,* servant. Some large Episcopal flocks are shepherded by an "executive priest." In our offices the first thing to go up on the wall is a tasteful arrangement of diplomas and, then, only if there is space, the crucifix.

But the proclamation of the word of God cannot be professionalized. It has no functional equivalents in secular culture. It cannot be camouflaged among socially useful or acceptable activities. Its passions are utterly nontransferable. The kerygmatic pitch, as Abraham Heschel said of the prophet's voice, is usually about an octave too high for the rest of society. If you are filling out a job application, see how far it gets you to put under *related skills:* "I can preach."

When ministers allow the word of God to be marginalized, they continue to speak, of course, and make generally helpful comments on a variety of issues, but they do so from no center of authority and with no heart of passion. We do our best to meet people's needs, but without the divine word we can never know enough or *be* enough, because consumer need is infinite. We are simply *there* as members of a helping profession. We annex to our ministry the latest thinking in the social sciences and preface our proclamations with phrases like "modern psychology tells us," forgetting that the word "modern" in such contexts usually indicates that what follows will be approximately one-hundred years out of date. What we lack in specialized knowledge we can only offset in time by making ourselves compulsively available to anyone in need.

I am convinced that no seminarian or candidate sets out to minister with such reduced expectations, and not everyone succumbs to this scenario, but ultimately the marginalization of the word of God fractions it into a hundred lesser duties.

The Gospel of Technology

The retreat from the word was fueled by the ideology of a newly professionalized culture and the personal insecurities of the minister. A second retreat from the word is underway, this one in large, successful churches whose members would never dream that the light-shows, videos, and PowerPoint presentations that accompany the Sunday sermon represent a fundamental lack of confidence in the spoken word of God. The new retreat is guided by a new professional class, the media and communications technicians whose expertise makes the sermon possible every Sunday. In many larger, media-oriented churches, the techies have become the most valuable members of the "sermon team," which includes a planning process in which the priestly encounter with the word of God has been displaced by something nearer a group engineering project.

When the legendary Lewis Gerstner became president of IBM he took over a company firmly in the grip of slide-ware style presentations. The standard format of any presentation relied on overhead projection. At his first big meeting at which one of the vice presidents was making such a presentation, Gerstner walked over to the projector and switched it off. Then, after a moment of stunned silence, he said, "Let's just talk about your business."[10]

I confess that when I visit some of the larger churches I want to flip off the switch to the PowerPoint and just talk about the Lord Jesus and our life together. One of the reasons I want to do this is that when the brain is asked to multi-task by listening and watching at the same time, it always quits listening. The spoken word possesses the greatest potential for communication in depth, but when the sound is turned off, the discourse moves quickly to the surface. Second, I don't believe the life of faith can be broken down into bullet points or that a logical or human connection between the bullet points can be demonstrated. The projected outline of the sermon gives the impression of a reasoned

10. Edward R. Tufte, *The Cognitive Style of PowerPoint* (Cheshire, Conn.: Graphics Press, 2003), p. 3. My criticisms of PowerPoint draw heavily on Tufte, who himself does not write in reference to religion or preaching.

flow of information, but the conversational, dialectical aspect of the sermon is eliminated. We are left with a list.

Kierkegaard said that it is not legitimate to ask a question in one medium and to answer it in another. If you want to experience Greek tragedy, you don't read about it in a comic book; you have to attend a play. Desire for the Eucharist cannot be satisfied by a lecture on the Eucharist. The Bible witnesses to a complex relationship between God and the world, one that includes ambiguity, suffering, and hope. Its profound questions of meaning cannot be answered by an ordered series of talking points. To do so is to falsify and cheapen divine revelation. How does one reduce to a series of bullet points Abraham's journey of faith, the Lord's agony in Gethsemane, or the psalmist's exuberant praise? What would Martin Luther King's "I Have a Dream" speech look like in PowerPoint?

My guess is that some preachers embrace technology because they recognize that the old communities of memory have broken down. What they may not understand is that the cords of memory have been cut by the very technology they are uncritically adopting. The small community that once faithfully gathered around altar and table is now shopping for a more comprehensive program. What holds many congregations together is not a tradition or a common religious experience but a style of consumption and a method of communication.

Ministers have not been slow to grasp the symbolic

value of technology in the church. The real benefits of projecting a clip from *Friends* or a series of bullet points on a screen are negligible. In themselves, these techniques only reproduce what we already have in our family rooms and offices. And that's the point! The very presence of such media serves to associate the sermon (and church and preacher) with the glamour, power, and authority of the same technology that rules the world. The medium really *is* the message. Technology is the new symbol of power. If the old symbol was the high pulpit and canopy, the new power-symbol is the remote in the shepherd's hand.

Several historians have noted that the older divisions among Christians based on doctrines such as justification, inspiration, or the Eucharist have given way to trans-denominational differences over social and political issues. It now seems clear that a new polarity is looming on the horizon, one that is technological in nature. It is already creating a great divide between those who embrace the myth of "perfect information at any given moment" and those who defy it, between those who wish to reinvent the sermon in the mirror of technology and those who continue to trust the spoken word.

Once again, the preacher stands at a vocational crossroads.

VOCATION

"A Vocation of Agony"

If we know anything about preaching, we know that whatever we do and however we do it is the result of a call. Remember, Martin Luther King said the *calling* to speak is a *vocation* of agony. He used these synonyms as if to remind us that it's not by accident or personal choice that we take up the word of God every Sunday. It is our vocation.[11]

When God created the world he did so by calling it into existence and naming it. All the metaphors are vo-

11. A number of studies enriched my understanding of vocation. Rowan Williams's two sermons on vocation in *A Ray of Darkness* ([Cambridge, Mass.: Cowley, 1995], pp. 147-59) are a good place to begin. Gary D. Badcock, *The Way of Life* (Grand Rapids: Eerdmans, 1998) is a theology of Christian vocation. Marie Theresa Coombs and Francis Kelly Nemeck, *Called by God* (Collegeville, Minn.: Liturgical Press, 1992), is a wide-ranging study focusing on the mystery of vocation. Brooks Holifield, *A History of Pastoral Care in America* (Nashville: Abingdon, 1983), traces the devolution of the Protestant ministry's vocation, and Robert Wuthnow, *After Heaven,* among his many works, explores the changing roles of clergy. Eugene H. Peterson organizes his treatment of vocation around the story of Jonah in *Under the Unpredictable Plant: An Exploration in Vocational Holiness* (Grand Rapids: Eerdmans, 1992). The best older studies include H. Richard Niebuhr, *The Purpose of the Church and Its Ministry* (New York: Harper, 1956), and Einar Billing, *Our Calling,* trans. Conrad Bergendoff (Philadelphia: Fortress, 1964 [1909]). Billing writes, "Life organized around the forgiveness of sins: that is Luther's idea of the call" (p. 18). Substitute "speech" for "life" and you have Luther's idea of the preacher's call. The specific vocational dimension of preaching is usually not included in treatments of the Christian's vocation.

cal. Then, in the ultimate act of power-sharing, the Lord also invited the man to join in the task of naming the creatures. Between them, they named the world into its wholeness and its stunning diversity. God's creative word is the origin of all vocations. Every creature has been given the ability to respond to the divine call, each according to its nature and gifts.

The Book of Genesis tells the story of the serpent's duplicity with words and the ensuing rupture in divine-human communication. Creation quickly lost the grace of vocation and along with it its ability to enter into a free and spontaneous dialogue with God. As Yeats put it, "The falcon cannot hear the falconer."

So God called again, this time in Jesus of Nazareth, who in his perfect faithfulness to the One who called, set the standard for responsive language.

Through Christ, God then created the *ecclesia,* the company of the called, in which believers continue to test and encourage one another's vocations.

The idea of vocation went on to develop a rich and complicated history, but recent evidence suggests that almost no one talks about their religious faith or daily work in terms of a response to God's call. "Vocation" is disappearing from our common vocabulary. Which leaves preachers in a particular bind because it's their vocation that gets them up in the morning and offers them a lifeline to purpose and power of expression. Call and response represents the basic rhythm of the preaching life.

Sometimes vocation is confused with a profession, as if anyone who has one of the historic professions in law or medicine automatically has a vocation. A profession once entailed an open and public commitment to the well-being of others. It required years of study and set the highest standards for admission to its ranks. Its rigorousness continues as a mark of health in any society. What we question in regard to the ministry is not its status as a profession but its vulnerability to professionalism, which is marked by a fascination with specialization, process, credentials, and measurable outcomes, the net effect of which is to undermine the minister's priestly and prophetic identity.

Theologically, what distinguishes a vocation from the rigors of a profession is this: you have to die to enter a vocation. A profession summons the best from you. A vocation calls you away from what you *thought* was best in you, purifies it, and promises to make you something or someone you are not yet.

In the Bible, God's call touches the most inviolable places in the human being. When God calls, you get a new name. You switch from Saul to Paul, from Simon to Peter. Once upon a time your name was "Emily," but now they call you "Preacher." You do not acquire a new gender or race, but these categories lose the definitive significance they claim in the wider culture. You give up your old family and gain a new one among whom you can speak freely. You are given a new ability, one that transfigures the old *dis*-abilities that once defined you as a person. It is significant that in the Old Testament God appoints as his chief spokesperson a stammerer. A vocation puts an end to you in order to disclose your true end.

No one understands this better than those who preach either from the margins of power or in defiance of it. In the 1930s two Fisk University scholars interviewed scores of ex-slave preachers and exhorters and recorded the stories of their call.[12] A single theme pervaded all the stories. The subjects reported they could not preach until something died in them and something new was born. The slaves died not only to their own sins but also to the oppression that kept them silent. But once they spoke, they did so with the jubilation of those set free from prison. They remembered it in a variety of ways, testifying to deep sorrow as well as the freedom of "unlocked jaws." An older woman evoked her call with the simple testimony, "God struck me dead."

Of course, not everyone comes to the preaching office by way of the Damascus Road. Some experience the gentler realization that their lives do not belong to them as fully as they once imagined. They cut the support lines that once connected them to cultural rewards. They let go of something. Their call, too, is marked by the grief of loss *and* the inexpressible joy of knowing that God wants them to speak.

12. Clifton H. Johnson, ed., *God Struck Me Dead* (Philadelphia: Pilgrim, 1969).

For those who are barred from religious office because of their gender, sexual orientation, or disability, the rhetoric of death has always posed a danger. Women, in particular, have repeatedly been told they must die to self, ambition, and will, only to be passed over for certain positions in the church — for their lack of ambition, drive, and will. For this reason women ministers are more likely than men to justify their presence in the pulpit on the basis of their call from God. For the rhetoric of the call does not crush the self or annihilate individual gifts but is prelude to a tremendous release of power. Women pastors continue to report that they experience the highest degree of freedom for ministry in the pulpit.[13] They say, in effect, "God seems to think I can preach!"

For preachers, as for all Christians, the journey from death to prophecy begins in baptism. Those who are baptized into Christ are baptized into his death, buried with him, so that just as he was raised from the dead, we too might walk — and *talk* — in newness of life. Our call follows the curve of his call.

Baptism signifies the death of one kind of language and the birth of another. As with all new vocations, this one brings with it the crisis of a new and unfamiliar vocabulary.

---

13. Carol M. Norén, *The Woman in the Pulpit* (Nashville: Abingdon, 1991), p. 16. On women's freedom in the pulpit, see pp. 46-48.

Terms we assumed would see us through to the end of our lives are wearing out. The old words like "self," "success," and "happiness" are not paying the dividends they once promised. The baptizand and congregation abjure the one who is associated with the old lies. "Do you renounce the devil and all his empty promises?" the baptismal liturgy asks, which is another way of asking, "Are you finished with the self-promoting, deceptive, violent, and godless discourses of this age?" And the congregation thunders as one, "We renounce them." God's people are promising to help this child inhabit a new linguistic world, one in which pride, hate, lying, and insincerity will have no place. Because of the niceties of the cultural ceremony, however, we fail to hear the slave's cry, "God struck me dead!"

The baptismal dynamic was present in the ministry of Martin Luther King Jr., who was one of those rare people in whom we see our vocations with greater clarity. In the days of black-church bombings in the South, King and his associates would often rush to the scene of a bombing and hold a service of prayer and preaching in the still-smoldering foundation. Several years ago I interviewed a few of the people who participated in these services. To each I posed the question, "What did he say?" And each responded, in effect, "I don't remember what he said, but I will never forget *where* he said it." Preaching in the ruins was his way of symbolizing the triumph of the word of God over every attempt to destroy it. The word from the ashes testified to his and the whole church's experience of death and resurrection.

Paul portrays the ministry of the word as a continuous action of being put to death and being renewed every day, as if pastoral care consists of thousands of mini-funerals and mini-Easters, moments of truth when this cancer or that divorce, this break-through or that triumph, puts the crucified and risen Lord right there with us on the razor's edge of ministry.

This is the mystic chain that connects suffering, action, hope, and words. All the disappointments and suffering represent the death of Jesus. The victories of hope and reconciliation, of unlocked jaws and really great sermons, of second winds and new beginnings, embody his resurrection from the dead.

Paul says it everywhere — in Romans, 1 Corinthians, and Galatians, but most powerfully in 2 Corinthians 2:12–6:11, as packed and rich a meditation on ministry as can be found anywhere. He writes, "For while we live we are always being given up to death for Jesus' sake, so that the life of Jesus may be manifested in our mortal flesh. . . . [D]eath is at work in us, but life in you" (4:11-12; cf. Col. 1:2). Later, in a typical 110-word sentence, Paul is pushing the envelope of language as he throws out image after ecstatic image of hard times on the mission circuit — calamities, beatings, imprisonments — when he blurts out, "We are treated . . . as dying — and look! — we live!" (6:9). Out of the ashes of disappointment, conflict, and a terrible salary comes the word of God for the people of God.

In the act of preaching something dies and something rises. What dies (or should die) is the preoccupation with the self that plagues so many performers. This death is ironic, since some sense of "self" is stimulated by God's call in the first place and is necessary for public speaking. The prophets are uniformly annihilated by a conversation with God, only to reappear as powerful individual performers of the word on God's behalf. They do not lack a sense of self.

So where do we draw the line between selflessness and the rather ample ego that characterizes so many public performers? Today's preachers are heirs to the twentieth-century mantra, "Be yourself!" Preaching is "truth through personality," but the two elements in Phillips Brooks's famous definition have become so entangled that they are indistinguishable from one another. And whenever there is a conflict between truth and personality, personality always wins.

In Book 4 of *On Christian Doctrine,* Augustine counseled preachers to subject their personal style to the rhetorical style of the text and the demands of the occasion. For example, you yourself may not be a particularly kerygmatic person, but the combination of Easter and a text from 1 Corinthians 15 will make you one. Even if you are not feeling doxological this Sunday, Paul's hymn to the majesty of God in Romans 11 will evoke a doxological sermon. When you lift your arms in praise, it is not really you who are doing that but the text, the Spirit, and the whole people of God moving in and through you. You and I might never choose to speak in so unprotected a manner ("that's not *me*"), but in the church that is the very speech that is given you and indeed reconstitutes "you" among the people of God.

What also dies in the act of preaching is the scavenger hunt for novelty that drives so many sermons, the antithesis of which was the ancient church's custom of preaching the homilies of others (and acknowledging their sources!). Later, the practice of borrowing was commonly carried out by untrained priests or in emergency situations by clergy who were unable to compose a suitable sermon, leading one historian to characterize medieval preaching as the art of using borrowed materials. The widespread use of helps and websites today, however, does not appear to represent fealty to the church's tradition or a crisis of training among the clergy. Rather, it reflects the preacher's need to compete with more effective and entertaining voices in a mass-media culture.

"The Church and I Were One"

What rises in the act of preaching? What rises is the remarkable synergy of the spoken word and the life of the baptized community, which in the parlance of Isaiah is the gift of a "new thing." It may not be possible for the speaker to become "consubstantial" with the audience, as one of my teachers used to counsel, but the spoken word is always aspiring to such communion. I have not found a livelier expression of this confluence of speaker and hearer than in the memoir of the novelist James Baldwin. In the essay "Down at the Cross," he is remembering his days as a boy preacher in a pentecostal church: "Nothing that has happened to me since equals the power and the glory that I sometimes felt when, in the middle of a sermon, I knew that I was somehow, by some miracle, really carrying, as they said, 'the Word' — when the church and I were one."[14]

When men and women take a deep baptismal plunge into ministry, they invariably surface as changed preachers. One pastor discovered the poor in his parish — not in some other neighborhood, but in his own parish — and his preaching took on new urgency. Another devoted herself to prayer for the sick as never before and began to speak with power she had never experienced. One discovered the ministry of his congregation as his wife lay dying, and in the midst of unspeakable sorrow he developed a new power to speak. Many a church's mission has loosed the tongue of its preacher.

The words of the sermon belong to the common life

---

14. James Baldwin, *The Fire Next Time* (New York: Dial, 1963), p. 47.

of God's people. The sermon emerges from the language of a believing community. It seems so obvious. But, as Robert Bellah has observed, our culture of radical individualism knows only two languages, facts and feelings, both of which claim to stand alone independent of any community.[15] Some preachers try to prove the "facticity" of the biblical record, dazzling their hearers with impressive data, while others build on issues raised by universal human experience (though rarely, it must be noted, does the human heart ask questions, the answers to which are *Trinity, cross, obedience, forgiveness*). Neither the conservatives nor the liberals capture the whole truth of the word.

Bonhoeffer and Barth broke the impasse long ago by boldly asserting the presence of the risen Christ within the linguistic community of the church. Bonhoeffer said the sermon is only Jesus pacing back and forth among his people. Barth said that the preacher stands between two Advents, the first and second comings of the Lord, by which he meant that because the risen Christ is alive and moving toward us from his own future, the preacher is not constrained to make him relevant as if Jesus were only a figure from the distant past. We do not have to prove that he is real because he is already here. We do not

15. Robert N. Bellah, "Christian Faithfulness in a Pluralist World," in *Postmodern Theology,* ed. Frederic B. Burnham (San Francisco: Harper and Row, 1989), p. 75.

have to dig him up from his *Sitz im Leben,* for the movement of preaching is not backward to the historical Jesus but forward toward the risen Christ. The first-person "I Am Judas" or "My Name is Mary Magdalene" genre of sermon lays excessive strain on the listener's imagination and the preacher's dramatic ability. To paraphrase P. T. Forsyth, preaching is the gospel taking this age seriously, not pretending that we belong to another.[16]

The point of preaching is not to go back but to meet the Lord out ahead. Training in preaching begins with training for ministry. "When did we see you naked or hungry or in prison?" the naive sheep ask the Judge. Preachers have ransacked nature, history, and their own emotions for illustrations of the divine. They have scratched into every conceivable experience in search of divinity or its analogues. They have explored every possible site except the very places Jesus promises to be — among those who suffer and seek restoration.

Preachers have looked for him virtually everywhere save among the ordinary practices of the people of God, who yearn more deeply than they are willing to admit for sermons that credibly portray *their* lives of faith — not Mother Teresa's, Gandhi's, or Gandolf's, but theirs. "If one wishes to promote the life of language," writes the poet

16. P. T. Forsyth, *Positive Preaching and the Modern Mind* (Grand Rapids: Baker, 1980 [1907]), p. 19. Forsyth's original 1907 publication was entitled *Positive Preaching and Modern Mind.*

Wendell Berry in *Standing by Words*, "one must promote the life of the community" in which the language flourishes.[17]

One Sunday in our congregation we baptized a baby the day after its mother's funeral. You don't have to be a professor of homiletics to wonder what the preacher will say in such a moment. Normally, our pastor never left the pulpit, but on that Sunday he did. I can still see him, the baby cradled in the crook of his arm, as he preached while pacing up and down the center aisle, as if to reinforce Bonhoeffer's definition of the sermon as Christ moving among his people. He tearfully claimed the promise of God for the child, and sternly reminded us of our responsibility toward her. The community responded to this intense, ambulatory sermon by vowing to care for the child. Technically, it was not a perfect sermon, only the right sermon for us. That morning the church and the word were one.

There is a goodness about the preaching office that transcends individual performance. Preaching is the ultimate vocation because at this the end of the age when so many sit stupefied and traumatized, the word gives power both to those who hear and to those who speak. It will save your life.

17. Wendell Berry, *Standing By Words* (San Francisco: North Point, 1983), p. 34.

The True End of Words

We cannot reverse the massive trends in communication or rescue the profession of ministry from social decline, but we can embrace our vocation. We can preach. And the vocation, since it comes from God, will make of us a sign in a world unsure of its responsibility and in a culture that treats language with loose indifference. In their sermons, preachers act as model responders for the church and world. They listen to God's word on behalf of others and, in the face of cultural interference, make bold reply. They bring up awkward subjects no one else is talking about. They speak of matters in the local church that one day the whole world will confess.

Preachers are authorized to say things that if they did not utter them no one would ever hear, except the stones cried out. Laments, blessings, oracles, doxologies. Where do you go to hear such talk? To what channel or court or classroom? Only in the community of faith. These forms of language require God as their final audience. They presuppose the creature's ability to respond to its creator and testify to the ultimate purpose of speech, which is to reflect the holiness of God and to effect reconciliation among God's creatures.

Sometimes preachers cannot help but envy other users of words in our culture. News anchors, analysts, comics, pundits, and savants: They are so smooth. They have but to open their mouths and out flows the spirit of the age. They are so professional that they are able to deliver gut-wrenching information without a hint of emotional investment, and all with an air of effortless familiarity. Next to them, the preacher often appears to be fighting off a swarm of bees. Why? Because preachers are speaking from the embedded position. Because their language emerges from pastoral participation in the life and death struggles of the baptized. Speaking of the apostle Paul, who by any account we have of him was not a smooth man, Joseph Sittler said: "Where grammar cracks, grace erupts." He adds a stern warning to preachers: "What God has riven asunder, let no preacher too suavely join together."[18]

Preaching is the ultimate vocation because it will save the lives of others. The public nature of vocation is taken up by Alasdair MacIntyre in his influential book *After Virtue,* in which he reminds us that certain classic roles once functioned as highly visible models of the moral life. These roles were filled by persons whose lives seemed to fit them perfectly. Such persons MacIntyre calls "characters."[19] In a character, no distinction exists between the role and the qualities of the person who exercises it. Society looks to these characters for guidance, for around them cluster important virtues and instruc-

18. Joseph Sittler, *The Ecology of Faith* (Philadelphia: Fortress, 1961), pp. 56-57.

19. Alasdair MacIntyre, *After Virtue,* 2nd ed. (Notre Dame, Ind.: University of Notre Dame Press, 1984), p. 31.

tive traditions. For example, in the United States we have an ongoing debate over what constitutes effective public education and decent health care only because the ideal character of the teacher or doctor is still etched on the public imagination. As the ideal lawyer Atticus Finch puts it in *To Kill a Mockingbird,* "I can't live one way in town and another way in my home."

Today's public characters are being superseded by hidden functions. The career bureaucrat and the software designer may be no less professional in their expertise, but they are largely hidden from view. The classic professions were never merely public performances; they were public standards by which others could take the measure of their vocation.

Many preachers chafe against the conventional mask they are expected to wear. They crave the interval of disinterest, the moment when they can be someone other than "the Reverend," a stolen moment, at least, when they (and their families) can cease to be spot-lit advocates of the truth. None of us wants to be absorbed into a role or ruled by a public persona, no matter how honorable and holy. Like Hazel Motes, we don't want to be called "preacher" or reduced to a social function. We would rather not be "set apart for the gospel" if it means the loss of personal autonomy.

A professional, after all, *can* live one way in town and quite another at home. Indeed, it is the mark of the professional that he or she can get the job done even in the midst of marital crises, financial problems, or other forms of personal chaos. Ministers, too, tend to be performance-oriented in the way the they view their work. They understand they are the products of a long process of formation, but they also know their job has its big days and special moments when they are unavoidably *on*. Like other professionals, they can step in and out of a role as easily as entering and exiting the sanctuary. But in the last analysis, the pastoral *character* humbly offers itself as a paradigm for the service, worship, and witness to God that belongs to all believers. It's not better performances the church needs, but truer characters.

The proclamation of the gospel is a vocation which by its very existence tells the world something about *its* vocation, even when the world has forgotten or does not want to hear. When a young black preacher stands up in the ashes of a Georgia church and announces the kingdom of God, that act momentarily re-casts the world. It represents to the world *another* world. It is a partial act to be sure, as evanescent as sound, and therefore must be repeated over and over, from one generation to the next, each making its passionate but partial witness to another world.

Our baptismal call remains the same, but the vocation to preach changes over time. Perhaps you were called to the heroic image of preaching as the prow of the ship, as Melville graphically depicts it in *Moby Dick,* but now find yourself doing the less visible work of speaking in the nursing home or the local prison. In form and venue, preaching has a constantly mutating quality that reflects the restless freedom of God and makes of it the ultimate postmodern activity. Disdaining grand truths, systems, metaphysics, and proofs, it revels in the fragmentariness of its own art. It trusts the slimmest of evidence. Among the poets its patron saint must be Emily Dickinson, who wrote, "Tell all the Truth but tell it slant. . . ./The Truth must dazzle gradually/Or every man be blind."

What else can the God who has been pushed onto a cross yield but glimpses of redemption offered by imperfect men and women to those with eyes to see? What else can these thin slices of literature called "texts" reveal but slants of light and vivid for-instances of something so brilliant that if we saw it whole it would kill us?

The work of preaching is carried out by men and women who are both tormented and comforted by the knowledge that next week and the week after, they will begin where they always begin, at the end of words, armed only with the conviction, "We can preach."

That there is such a vocation in this world means there is hope for all of us.

INTERPRETATION

Chapter Two

The Final Edition

Every preacher's Bible has seen better days. The leather that was supposed to last a lifetime is seriously cracked and worn; the spine has been thoughtlessly flexed at too many graves and garden weddings. Its delicate pages have been folded down and creased for future reference — a proverb one had no idea existed, a Psalm that unexpectedly moved the heart. Now they simply refuse to lie flat. Some of its verses are illegible, the result of inspirations inscribed in pen when a pencil wasn't available. It is not an attractive book anymore, flagged as it is with scraps of paper and ragged bookmarks on which one can still make out the hastily jotted prayer or the outline of an impromptu meditation. There are names on these scraps, too, and seeing them evokes a face, an emotion, or the fragment of some all-but-forgotten story of ministry. They are all in the book.

One of the great joys of ministry is that it entails so much required reading, a lifetime of imaginative reading, to be exact. Like all Christians, the minister is a creature of the book, but with a crucial difference. Most believers read the Bible and as a result something of the Spirit's message makes its home in them. They are informed, inspired, indwelt, and ultimately changed by what they have read. But unlike most Christians through whom the book passes into thought and behavior, the preacher takes this love affair with the Bible one step further. The preacher reads the book, then speaks it. The text passes from heart and mind through the lips of the speaker and emerges into an assembly of people. "The word is near you," says Paul, "on your lips and in your heart."

This is the nub of our inquiry, then, not how to read the Bible for increase in knowledge or guidance in ethics, which the Bible bestows along with many other blessings, but how to read it as a prelude to preaching.

Where Do You Read?

When we open the book to interpret it, the first thing we encounter is other interpreters, not unlike ourselves, assessing ancient texts for their contemporary meaning. It's like looking at a portrait of someone painting a portrait.

The Gospels portray Jesus as one who was deeply involved in interpretive conversations from the time he was a twelve-year-old in the temple to the evening of his resurrection when he appeared on the Emmaus Road. In

Luke 10, for example, we come upon an exegetical discussion between Jesus and a lawyer. When the lawyer quizzes him about an important religious issue, Jesus refers the man to the Scripture they hold in common and asks, "What is written in the law? How do you read?" This is a familiar set-up in the New Testament: "Is it not written?" "What do the Scriptures say?" "Have you not read?"

What usually follows such a question is a radical re-reading of the Scripture in support of a radical new truth. Radical because the old stories are being transfigured by a new time-frame, that of the in-breaking of the end of time. What was once good, holy, and somewhat old news has suddenly become the final edition of that same news but now utterly transformed. The final edition is Jesus re-reading Isaiah from the perspective of the end of history. It is Paul explaining the ultimate significance of Abraham to Jewish Christians. It is Matthew repeatedly announcing the completion of that which, before Jesus, might have needed no completion.

What is written? How do you read? The first question has to do with what lawyers would call black letter law: What is found in the statutes and common law? The second question, the *how* question, has to do with interpretation, performance, and the habit of thinking like a lawyer (or a preacher): How do you read? That is, What are we to make of it? What does it mean in this instance?

After two thousand years, plus three in seminary, we know *what* is written. We can make out the black marks on the white page. But from early Monday morning to late Saturday night, the preacher never stops worrying the second question, How do you read?

Biblical interpreters have often answered the "how" question by means of a "what." Fundamentalists have celebrated the character of the *book* with all its perfections, as if to suggest that the objective accuracy and clarity of the book leave little room for differences of interpretation. In similar fashion, liberals have examined the character of the *world* in which the book was produced in order to ponder crucial matters of interpretation. Given what we know about the violent, patriarchal, pre-scientific prejudices that shaped the world in which the Bible was written, how can it speak authoritatively to us? What can it possibly offer, they ask, beyond confirmation of a few universal principles? But as Luke Timothy Johnson has admonished, "If scripture is ever again to be a living source for theology, those who practice theology [and preach] must become less preoccupied with the world that produced scripture and learn again how to live in a world scripture produces. This will be a matter of imagination, and perhaps of leaping."[1] Both approaches to Scripture — one focused on the attributes of the book, the other on the attributes of the world in which the book

1. Luke Timothy Johnson, "Imagining the World Scripture Imagines," in *Theology and Scriptural Imagination*, ed. L. Gregory Jones and James J. Buckley (Oxford: Blackwell, 1998), p. 3.

was produced — remove the Bible from its native habitat in the church's worship, catechesis, and pastoral care. They take it out of the only world in which it has a chance to make sense.

Most church people instinctively know that the Bible is not a perfect book. They also know that it offers them more than a few guiding principles. For them the Bible is a trusted and wise friend who never lets them down. It is *Scripture.* How often in the lobby of a hospital or on the elevator doesn't the pastor make one last check of the Psalm of the day before entering the ward? And the parishioner, though frightened and weakened by illness, whispers the Psalm along with her pastor and takes refuge in it.

Church people instinctively take the measure of their lives in the mirror of the Bible's personages and teachings. A man struggles heroically with his wife's illness and related personal and financial problems, only to be stricken with heart disease himself. This is the last straw. He codifies his fate in the company of a fellow sufferer. "I must be Job," he says. On a larger scale, entire peoples have survived only by reading their history figurally, as a distant rhyme or replay of another people's struggle for deliverance from bondage or persecution. Over the centuries, more than one prophet has merged his voice with Moses' "Let my people go!"

Preachers engage the hermeneutical task formally, parishioners less formally, but both never cease making connections between realities portrayed in the Bible and the events of their own lives. When Christians gather for worship, their liturgy, prayers, readings, and hymns are saturated with the language-world of the Bible, which they embrace as normative for their understanding of themselves and God. They name their churches Ebenezer, Gilead, Mount Bethel, or New Macedonia and merge their identities with the shrines and communities of the Bible.

The church is the social location in which the New Testament was written and in which the majority of Christians still reads it. If the preacher is looking for an alternative to the fundamentalism that worships the book and the liberalism that marginalizes it, let him or her listen to how the people of God actually use the Bible on their better days. The Bible is best interpreted on location by those who consider themselves active players in its drama. What interpretive precision they lose by a lack of objectivity they more than regain by their intuitive practice of identification.

Following the work of theologian George Lindbeck, it has become fashionable to talk about how the life-stories of believers are absorbed into the biblical story. To be the people of God means to live in the Bible's story-world and to be governed by the Bible's language game.[2] Lindbeck's theory is ideally true but practically false. The problem is,

2. George Lindbeck, *The Nature of Doctrine* (Philadelphia: Westminster, 1984).

as most pastors know, that many of the people of God are either enmeshed in competing stories or are unacquainted with the biblical story in which they are supposed to be living.

In my last pastorate I was disappointed to discover that of my twenty-nine catechism students — sons and daughters of the Reformation all, mere weeks away from lifelong status as "dyed-in-the-wool Lutherans" — only one knew the answer to the question, "What did Jesus say to the thief on the cross who believed in him?" The students certainly felt they were enrolled in something called "church," but their knowledge of its scripts was limited. Perhaps it is not critically important that Christians know their Bible chapter and verse. But surely in some distant nursing home, hospital, prison, or personal crisis, those kids, who are now in their mid thirties, might well want to rely upon the exact words of one of the most glorious promises in the New Testament.

It is not literacy for its own sake that we are after but the larger, Lindbeckian sense of the community, whose ordinary language shapes the lives and habits of its members. Reading the Bible is more like learning a language than translating a few phrases. When you really know a language, translation is unnecessary. The learner may proudly say, "I don't know when it happened, but I just noticed I am thinking in Spanish!" How do you read the Bible in such a way that you quit translating and begin to think and speak in its language?

How Do You Read?

In conversations with a terminally ill friend, I noticed that she read the Bible differently than I and radically so. As a matter of theological principle we both acknowledged the importance of the gospel in the Bible, but she clung to it and claimed it as her personal prize. My friend read the Bible with an evangelical tenacity that allowed her to discover the promise of God in any passage, even those whose surface details seemed far removed from the gospel. Her theological instincts told her that the Bible was preserved as a testimony to God's faithfulness. Reading it was an everyday exercise in praying and claiming and being claimed, which is what it should be for everyone who opens the book, even busy preachers. My friend would have seconded the comment by the poet Adrienne Rich: "Read," she said, "as if your life depended on it."[3]

A great deal has been written about the existential and moral commitment implied in the act of reading. Rich's comment, which is not made in reference to Scripture, is a case in point. She counsels the reader "to allow what you are reading to pierce the routines, safe and impermeable, in which ordinary carnal life is tracked, charted, channeled." While I cannot prove what I am about to say, I suspect that the near-religious value with

3. Adrienne Rich, *What Is Found There* (New York: Norton, 1993), p. 32.

which literary critics invest the act of reading is learned from ordinary Jews and Christians who love their Scripture. "I wonder," asks a character in a Chaim Potok novel, "if Gentiles clasp Holy Scripture in their arms and dance with it, as we Jews do?" Who first read the word with so total an investment of the self? Who first "ate" the word? Who finally incarnated it?

In the library of Gettysburg College in Gettysburg, Pennsylvania, they can show you the bloodstains in their books. The stains run deep in their pages because in the battle so many were wounded that the nurses ran out of pillows. So they took books from the shelves in the library and laid the heads of the wounded on them. The church's book, too, is stained and penetrated by the cost of God's love. From beginning to end, the entire New Testament witnesses to the cost. That is why we read it — because our lives do depend on it.

The most important hermeneutical category is not sociological, psychological, or political — but theological. We read the Bible evangelically (if I may reclaim a precious word that belongs to all Christians), not because it is filled with good stories but because it radiates good news about the character and disposition of God. The gospel is the account of God's turning toward us in Jesus Christ, the idea being that the last thing human beings need is a god who turns *away* from us at critical moments or in desperate situations. God is *for* us and has promised to be so for Israel, the church, the poor, and the outsider. Such a statement is not so much a litmus test for identifying "the poor" or the "outsider" as it is a testimony to God's character as it is revealed in the Bible. When you really catch on to the promise in the Bible, or, as my former teacher Robert Bertram used to say, when you read a text in such a way that it *necessitates* Christ, then the purpose of Scripture is clarified, and you are almost ready to preach.

The preacher is like a gemologist who turns a precious stone this way and that in order to capture its brilliance, much in the way the rabbis sought to bring out the "perfection" of the text. The interpreter/preacher rotates the passage against the light, viewing it from every angle until it discloses the glory of God, which for the believer has already been revealed in the face of Jesus Christ.

I embrace this evangelical hermeneutic as a gift of freedom for the preacher. It is in Religion 101 that we first learn to view the Bible as a problem. There we are reintroduced to this book — the one we grew up with! — as if it were an alien document that cannot possibly be understood except by means of various tools and specialized information. In too many seminaries, too, the introductory Bible courses are a form of hazing of the uninitiated. They produce cynicism toward the text precisely where one would expect reverence. Instead of beginning with the truth of God's faithfulness and adopting that as a reliable reading-guide, the beginner is first trained to identify the many factors that make the Scripture problematic and distance it from modern people like us, which include the patriarchy, chauvinism, violent behavior, and primitive worldview of those who either wrote the book or appear as characters in its pages.[4] These factors are serious and must be taken into account in interpretation, but if we start from them or allow them to norm our reading, it is difficult if not impossible to arrive at a receptivity to the true character of God. Instead of witnessing *to* God, the Scripture inadvertently witnesses *against* God and makes it harder rather than easier for the reader to believe. The preacher winds up apologizing for God, the way spin doctors tell us what the candidate *really* meant, rather than proclaiming the justice, love, joy, and peace whose true source is the God of Israel and Jesus — the God of the Bible.

Of course, the Bible *is* a culturally distant book. As someone has said, reading the Pauline epistles is like opening other people's mail. These letters don't appear to be addressed to us at all. The writer and addressees often seem to be operating with a hidden agenda. We can understand each word; it's the sentences that confuse us!

Several years ago, our family found a letter written long

4. See Richard B. Hays, "Salvation by Trust? Reading the Bible Faithfully," *The Christian Century* 114, no. 7 (26 February 1997): 218-23. Reprinted under the title "A Hermeneutic of Trust" in *The Company of Preachers,* ed. Richard Lischer (Grand Rapids: Eerdmans, 2002), pp. 265-74.

ago by my great-grandfather to my great-grandmother. It contained this sentence: *"Surely, Miss Laura, you are not insensible of the constraints which both nature and fortune have laid upon me in the matter of our mutual necessity."* Here the historical-critical method is indispensable. What *did* nineteenth-century Kentuckians mean when they spoke of "mutual necessity"? That was code for what? Consider these words of Paul to the Corinthians: "I have been a fool! You forced me to it. Indeed you should have been the ones commending me, for I am not at all inferior to these super-apostles, even though I am nothing." To which we add, "Word of God for the people of God."

Contrast these problems with the conviction of early medieval scholars who, says Beryl Smalley, "thought of Scripture as a letter addressed to them by God."[5] Many Christians have honored the "oracular" power of Scripture, by which individuals hear the word as if the usual laws of literary transmission were suspended and it was addressed to them alone.[6] One thinks of Augustine, who, deep in his crisis of faith, hears a child cry, *Tolle, lege,* "Pick it up, read it." He flings open his copy of the Pauline epistles and is transformed by what he reads. Dietrich Bonhoeffer was reading other people's mail in New York City in 1939, more specifically, Timothy's mail from Paul,

5. Beryl Smalley, *The Study of the Bible in the Middle Ages* (Oxford: Clarendon, 1941), p. 27.

6. James L. Kugel and Rowan A. Greer, *Early Biblical Interpretation* (Phildelphia: Westminster, 1986), p. 193.

"Do your best to come before winter," which Bonhoeffer decoded as a message addressed to him and quickly returned to Germany and to death.

Both the culturally distant and the oracular views of the text represent extreme understandings of how the Bible operates. The first excessively limits what we can learn from an ancient and alien document. The second, the oracular, exaggerates the reach of the text by attributing to it a laser-like ability to find its targets one heart at a time.

If preachers must choose between these two options, let them err on the side of the laser beam. Preaching consists in just such an improbable dramatic encounter between God and the hearer, one in which the hearer senses that he or she is being directly *addressed,* when the "you" of Romans or Galatians magically becomes the "you" of this gathered moment. In his preface to his Christmas sermons, *A Brief Introduction on What to Look for and Expect in the Gospels,* Luther instructs the reader or the listener to pretend that they are standing before the living Christ. How do you read? This is his answer:

> When you open the book containing the Gospels and read or hear how Christ comes here or there, or how someone is brought to him, you should therein perceive the sermon or the gospel through which he is coming to you, or you are being brought to him. For the preaching of the gospel is nothing else than Christ

coming to us, or we being brought to him. When you see how he works, however, and how he helps everyone to whom he comes or who is brought to him, then rest assured that faith is accomplishing this in you and that he is offering your soul exactly the same sort of help and favor through the gospel. If you pause here and let him do you good, that is, if you believe that he benefits and helps you, then you really have it.[7]

How does this hermeneutical key offer freedom to the preacher? When you "really have it," as Luther said, there is no fundamental discrepancy between your identity and your interpretive acts. You are what you read. When you really do have a view of the God of salvation, you cannot utterly misinterpret the biblical text, a claim which admittedly lays itself open to abuse. Nevertheless, you cannot get it completely wrong about God. Why? Because in its offer of life, the text is making a true and measurable "print" in the life of the interpreter. It is replicating itself in the reader.

This hermeneutic of generosity suggests practical implications for the organization of a sermon. It means that the preacher reads the text for its *evangelical insight* and shapes the sermon according to its dynamic. The interpreter gathers as much knowledge as possible from the

7. *Luther's Works*, vol. 35, ed. E. Theodore Bachmann (Philadelphia: Fortress, 1960), p. 121.

text and then proceeds to locate the moment of transaction or transformation in the text by which the Holy Spirit is moving the hearer from one condition, understanding, or way of life to another. Locating this move is an exercise of the imagination, which in homiletics is too often limited to "picturing" what life must have been like in first-century Palestine or inserting apt illustrations of familiar truths. The theological imagination listens to the whole text, appraises it, enjoys it, and then prescinds from it the shape of God's empowerment in Jesus Christ, which provides the sermon its only wedge into the contemporary consciousness.

What I am describing is the angle, slant, or what Germans used to call the *Winkel,* from which the preacher approaches every sermon. The word *Winkel* has passed into the English language as a seldom-used verb, "to winkle." Thus we might say the preacher winkles out the text until its life-changing power is disclosed. This is hard work, the hardest work connected with preaching, because not every text gives up its *Winkel* without a fight. For this reason Luther offered the doctor's cap to anyone who consistently gets it right.

I focus on the evangelical insight, or the *generous* method of reading, in contrast to at least three popular homiletical approaches to interpreting the text: the *flat, convenient,* and *ironic* readings of Scripture.

The *flat reading* approaches every text in verse-by-verse fashion on the unspoken assumption that the content of each verse is as important and helpful as that of every other verse in the text. Consequently, it tends to miss the theological and emotional curve of the text. The sermons it produces lend themselves to teaching a variety of lessons in serial form but at the expense of the whole text's transforming power.

Adherents of the School of Flat Reading have always claimed that their method eliminates the biases and artistic flights of the interpreter. One simply takes the truth from the text the way broadcasters read their cue cards. But no one reads the Bible by any method whatsoever without the use of a filter or what Calvin called "spectacles" that give clarity and color to the reader's conclusions. What we actually have is a series of filters superimposed upon one another, which includes but is not limited to our experience, context, race, gender, class, and most of all, our convictions about how God is present to us in the world — our theology. No hermeneutic can do away with these very human filters without doing away with the humanity of the reader as well. Nevertheless, the flat reading appeals to many preachers who, finding themselves stuck for something to say or unwilling to do the hard, synthetic work of the theological imagination, fall back on verse-by-verse explanation as the "most faithful" method of biblical interpretation.

The next alternative I call the *convenient reading* of the text. It has no difficulty finding useful ideas in the text; the only problem is they do not arise from the text's center in the gospel. For example, if Jesus wept over his friend Lazarus, perhaps it is also good for us to show our emotions more freely. If Jesus turned over the money-changers' tables, perhaps we too ought to express our anger at injustice. If the Master could call lowly tax-collectors and prostitutes into the kingdom, surely we too can recognize the potential of unlikely people. The interpreter reads and rereads the text until a usable notion pops out, often one that has political, psychological, or cultural currency. This is a convenient method of reading because the Bible brims with so many fascinating insights into history and human nature that the preacher can pick the closest one at hand. In so doing, however, he or she may be lured away from the overriding purpose of Scripture, which is to save people from sin, form them for community, and equip them for lives of discipleship in the world.

The final alternative and the most difficult of the approaches to explain is the *ironic reading* of Scripture. Unlike the convenient reading, it makes much of the greatness of God and the importance of the Bible but often at the expense of God's saving grace. The preacher consistently demonstrates the inferiority of everything human to the divine, which is true enough, but never gets round to God's identification with humankind in Jesus Christ. This approach focuses on the distance between God and humanity but does little to bridge the gap. Humanity appears doomed to live in the ironic discrepancy between its own pretensions and the majesty of God. The only dimension of the divine-human relationship the preacher explores is that of an unrelieved tension. Every Sunday the hearer leaves church chastened but never healed. The ironic method is often mistaken for prophetic preaching, but this is a slur on Jeremiah and his cohort, for however much the prophets critiqued Israel they never failed to announce God's pity for the poor and his mercy to those who repent.

The three methods I have outlined — the *flat, convenient,* and *ironic* readings of Scripture — make what is essentially a moral contribution to the sermon. These three may suggest some instructive statements of truth, but because nothing in them (or the interpreter) dies and rises, they cannot produce the tautness of a genuinely theological sermon. They fall flat.

So far, you might have noticed some circularity in the argument of this chapter. We read the Scripture through the lens of God's faithfulness. But how can we begin with God's character as a hermeneutical guide when it is precisely God's character that one hopes to discover by reading the Bible? When you read the book, are you already supposed to know the ending?

Yes, but how?

With Whom Do You Read?

One of the many pleasant things about reading to children is that they need you to be there for both the happy and the scary parts of the story. It is permissible for you to be amazed by events, but not too amazed, scared by villains and monsters, but not so scared that your little co-readers doubt for their safety. Children want to read with someone who has already been through the material, who is thoroughly acquainted with every surprising twist in the story and who can guarantee its ending for them. They want to read with someone they trust.

We read the Bible in the company of those who have already experienced its surprises and twists and who know its glorious ending. We read with those who have told us in advance what to look for and expect when we open the book. We read with those who have taught and embodied the love of God in Jesus Christ. We read with the church — with our parents, grandparents, pastors, counselors, siblings, friends, and teachers — with the saints.

How do the saints read the Bible? The short answer is, Slowly, very slowly. In his book *Religious Reading,* Paul J. Griffiths makes a telling distinction between what he calls a *consumerist* method of reading the Bible and the *religious* reading.[8] If Adolf von Harnack said the

8. Paul J. Griffiths, *Religious Reading* (New York: Oxford, 1999), p. 47.

historian's duty is to get intellectual control of the object, the consumerist would add, "And as quickly as possible." The consumerist guts the book the way one cleans a fish, as swiftly and efficiently as can be done. We have limited time for the weekly exegesis, so limited, in fact, that we convince ourselves that we do not have time for praying the text, meditating upon its meaning for our own lives, or praying for our parishioners, unless, of course, such activities will produce a more effective sermon.

The religious reader is a slow reader. If anything gets gutted in reading, it will be the interpreter, not the text. The consumerist shines a flashlight on the text and says, "Tell me all you know." The religious reader allows the light of the text to illumine his or her own life and that of the congregation. "O Lord, thou hast searched me and known me." The religious reader already knows the ending, so he or she is free to enjoy the story.

Griffiths's distinctions help define the growing chasm between two powerful interpretive traditions: scientific criticism and theological exegesis. Many of us were schooled in the first. I define the second as biblical interpretation that is sifted through the life, doctrines, and practices of the community for which it was intended and in which it is practiced. Theological exegesis is the church reading its book. We read it as if it were addressed to our particular community and as if our lives depended on its conclusions, yet also in the conviction that its authority stretches well beyond our little congregation to the church of every time and place.

Not long ago I preached on the Ascension of the Lord. I had never preached on the ascension because, as everyone knows, Jesus ascended on a Thursday and we do not have church on Thursdays, which means that one can spend a lifetime in ministry without having to make sense of the ascending, triumphant Christ as he ends one ministry in the flesh and begins another in the power of the Spirit.

Why had I been so intimidated by this festival? Because I thought I had to explain how it happened in such a way that would satisfy modernist objections. Because I thought I had to demythologize it, then *re*theologize, or worse, moralize it, and finally apply it to contemporary life with no fewer than three gripping illustrations.

Despite my reluctance to tackle the ascension, the church routinely addresses it when it recites its rule of faith, *"He ascended into heaven and is seated at the right hand of the Father."* We say it every Sunday because it is written in our script, and if you do not speak the right lines, you may not be in the right story. You have not told the whole story of Jesus if you omit his resurrection from the dead and his ascension into heaven. The church confesses its faith not in order to explain the more obscure events in the life of Jesus, but to tell the whole story as fully as possible and to make a statement about its own identity in relation to it.

Furthermore, the church has chosen a strategy for "reading" the ascension of Jesus. It has appointed a Psalm, Psalm 47, by which to guide its response to this mysterious event. While I have heard sermons that read the ascension as an ominous foreshadowing of postmodern alienation, of the loneliness of humanity in a world bereft of God's presence, the Psalm appointed for worship on Ascension Day approaches the event in a different spirit. It preaches joy: "God has gone up with a shout, the Lord with the sound of a trumpet." Jesus had to "go away" in order to establish a more universal dominion. He had to ascend to the right hand of God, which Luther said means "everywhere."

God's supremacy over all would-be gods was originally performed by the king of Israel in the temple enthronement ritual. That triumph "happened again" when the Son of God ascended through the clouds, and "happens again" (present tense) when the church celebrates his victory in worship. Imagine the scene in the temple when the God of Israel, in the guise of the king, takes his place above the nations. Imagine it again when the Lord Jesus, with a host of captives in his train, enters heaven in triumph. Imagine it one more time when the people of God join him in the heavenly places.

The three scenes of enthronement are related as recurring figures in an elaborate tapestry. The ascension is not a lesson or a principle to be artificially divided, but an emblem of everything the church hopes and strives for.

Remember, the genius of the creed is that when we confess something about God, we are making a claim about our own destiny as well.

By connecting the elevation/ascension to God's rule over the nations, Psalm 47 and the book of Acts portray it as a political triumph. God has won the victory by overcoming the Son's spatial confinement in the world and replacing it with something far greater.

One Easter evening my wife and I were driving through one of the poorest and most depressed communities in eastern North Carolina. We passed a doublewide in the woods where someone had taken a piece of posterboard and made a little sign and planted it at the end of the driveway where everyone on the main road would have to confront it. Written in magic marker, it said, "The grave could not hold him." The sign read like roadside poetry at its best. It drew us and all passersby into an implicit conspiracy against the powers of death. *"Psst. The grave could not hold him. Pass it on."* Because he is risen and now ascended, he secretly rules everything. The Lord is now free to be everywhere.

The story of the ascension relativizes all the Herods, Agrippas, and tinhorn lords we will meet in the book of Acts. Luke has initiated a rolling critique of all earthly pretenders to authority, including those of our own day. In what follows, the whole tapestry of the church's mission will unfold beneath the canopy of the ascended

Lord. *God reigns in the face of death and politics,* Luke says. *Let the mission begin.*[9]

Does this ancient story *mean* all that? When you are reading with the church, the answer is always, "O yes, and much, much more."

The tapestried reading of the ascension outlined above is artlessly restrained in comparison with the church's rich habits of interpretation. The parables of Jesus are a case in point. I doubt there is a modern academic book on the parables that does not include a condescending reference to Augustine's famous allegorization of the parable of the Good Samaritan, in which Jericho stands for mortality, the priest and Levite the institutions of the old dispensation, the donkey Christ's human nature, the two coins present and future life, the inn the church, the innkeeper the apostle Paul, and so on. Modern scholars then warn their students not to fall into Augustine's mistakes. Now, aside from the questionableness of premising any approach to biblical interpretation on the errors of St. Augustine, we might want to rethink our blanket condemnation of allegory. The church read the story allegorically because that interpretation arose out of its own life with God. The medieval church used texts like stained glass windows, to emblazon

9. See Richard Lischer, "God Has Gone Up with a Shout!" in *Exploring and Proclaiming the Apostles' Creed,* ed. Roger E. Van Harn (Grand Rapids: Eerdmans, 2004), pp. 173-77.

the story of salvation. Its interpretations were powerful renderings designed to make the letter come alive.

Compare the figural interpretation with the single-point doctrine of modern nineteenth- and twentieth-century parable-theory, and the latter seems rather thin. As a seminarian, Martin Luther King Jr. preached on this parable, and, following his sources in mid-century liberalism, what he got out of it was that the parable teaches one truth and one truth only, namely, the importance of "altruism" in human relations. It is a disappointing sermon, if one is allowed to say that of Martin Luther King.

Not long before he died, King preached on another parable, "A Knock At Midnight" (from Luke), in which a neighbor troubles a friend for provisions. This time King allegorizes the story with no less floridity than Augustine, telling his congregation that *midnight* stands for socially troubled times like these; the *knock* at the door stands for the world asking the church for help; the *bread* stands for the spiritual nourishment that only the church can give; the neighbor's initial *disappointment* represents the world's disillusion with the church's moral failures. To this blatantly allegorical interpretation he adds a stunning climax in which he implores the church "to keep the bread fresh," that is, to guard the integrity of the message.[10] Now,

10. Both sermons are included in Martin Luther King Jr., *Strength to Love* (Philadelphia: Fortress, 1963). His peroration on keeping the

which was the truer interpretation, the universal appeal to altruism, which satisfies the demand for civil morality, or the figural appeal grounded in the church's mission?

Figural interpretation reminds us of the layered and woven character of preaching. The word "text" comes from the verb "to weave" — hence *textile*. Every text suggests several patterns of interpretation, and the preacher may weave a different one every year.[11]

Once we learn to read *with* the church, we will honor the church in our sermons. Linguistically, the sermon will create a symbolic world over time in which the reality of the people of God is central. It's odd, but we gather every Sunday as a group, pray for one another, receive the Eucharist shoulder to shoulder, and sing our hymns in unison. We read from a book that records the history of a people. But this togetherness is punctuated by a fifteen- or twenty-minute speech that is often dominated by appeals to universal truths or personal experiences.

The sermon is a word from one church to another

---

bread fresh is found only in the audiotapes and typescripts of one of the delivered versions of "A Knock At Midnight."

11. David Cunningham's investigation of Matthew 8:20, "Foxes have holes . . . ," unearths no fewer than nine distinct interpretations of that passage in the tradition, in *Faithful Persuasion* (Notre Dame, Ind.: University of Notre Dame Press, 1991), p. 231. See the multiple readings of the Parable of the Workers in the Vineyard (Matt. 20:1-16) cited by David C. Steinmetz, "The Superiority of Pre-Critical Exegesis," in *The Theological Interpretation of Scripture,* ed. Stephen E. Fowl (Oxford: Blackwell, 1997), pp. 26-38.

mediated by the common use of Holy Scripture. It is a church word. Many of us, however, instinctively remove the scandal of the church from the sermon. In our sermons the gospel is confirmed by appeals to psychology, politics, sports, and personal experience but at the expense of the community's own life as the body of Christ. We preach *in* churches of course, but rarely do we tell the story *of* the church with a vividness and goodness of its own.

Too many preachers continue to believe that something called "human nature" forms the hermeneutical bridge between the many generations separating the biblical world and our own. But is it really true that no matter how distant we are from our ancestors, we all share in an ideal essence of humanity unconditioned by history or changing worldviews? Is *that* what really makes us brothers and sisters to David, Ruth, Peter, Paul, and the Corinthians? It should be that easy! We have enough difficulty recognizing the humanity of our contemporaries of other races, sexual orientations, and nationalities to warn us away from placing our confidence in a trans-generational bond of human nature.

The common denominator between Christians is not human nature but the church, which, as always, can be found gathered around lectern and pulpit, where it listens attentively for a word from the Lord, and scattered throughout the world, where it attempts to perform the word with integrity.

How Do You Preach What You Have Read?
A Comment on Style

I began this chapter by saying that the preacher takes his or her relationship with Scripture one step farther than most Christians by speaking the book. When you read the great texts, you realize they not only want to be lived, they also want to be spoken. But how? Here the question of style enters the arena of biblical interpretation.

Modern preachers have inherited an impoverished notion of style from the ancients. They defined style as the verbal projection of one's personal qualities. "Style is the person," they said. Add to their wisdom the truisms of modern psychology, and we have a notion of style that is intimately related to the discovery of one's authentic personality. Since we have only one ego — or so goes this line of reasoning — we can speak in only one style. Ask most preachers what they strive for stylistically, and the majority will reply, "To be *myself* in the pulpit."

But must our verbal key signature emerge from some hidden monolith called "the person"? In classical thought the word "person" meant the opposite of our concept of permanent identity. The *persona* was the mask through which the actor spoke (hence *per-sonar,* "sounded through"). The actor's style depended on the contours of the mask, the role, and the audience's need to hear the lines clearly.

Even in preaching, style belongs on the surfaces of

things. The preacher makes adjustments in matters of diction (word choice), figures of speech, and manner of speech *not* on the basis of his or her personality or mood but in deference to the nature of the text and the demands of the occasion. Even the most introverted cleric will become, *must* become, a trumpet on Easter Sunday. The kerygma does not emerge from anything deep within our selves.

In an era when *style* was actually taught in schools, Augustine created a revolution in homiletics by counseling preachers *not* to be themselves. He said, in effect, perhaps your *self* should not dominate every text and every liturgical occasion, for each text of Scripture has its own style and therefore suggests the manner in which it should be preached. Only a former professor of rhetoric could have made such an argument. Following Cicero, he recognized three basic styles of expression: the *low,* which instructs the audience; the *moderate,* which entertains; and the *grand,* which moves the heart and soul.[12]

Sometimes the text wants you to be a teacher or a maker of arguments. Its own style counsels you to be patient and reflective. In Galatians 4:21, Paul says, "Tell me, you who desire to be under the law, do you not hear the

12. The following discussion is taken entirely from Book 4 of *On Christian Doctrine.* The scriptural examples are Augustine's. For a modern theory of style that is indirectly related to Augustine, see Richard A. Lanham, *Style: An Anti-Textbook* (New Haven: Yale University Press, 1974).

law?" and you can almost see Professor Paul gazing thoughtfully at his congregation over his half-spectacles.

But other texts from the very same apostle to you, the very same personality, suggest very different stylistic strategies. The following words of the apostle suggest a "moderate" or delightfully elegant style. Why? Because Paul's use of balanced phrases and antitheses *is* elegant and a delight to the ear. His words are designed to entice the hearer rather than overpower him. "Bless those who persecute you; bless and do not curse them. Rejoice with those who rejoice, weep with those who weep . . ." (Rom. 12:14-15). One senses that in the rhythm of his prose the apostle is trying to capture the rhythm of the Christian life.

Augustine also identified passages written in the "grand style," whose purpose is to touch the soul and move the hearer to new levels of discipleship. Some passages invite even the PowerPoint-prone preacher to soar like a poet — or a lawyer! Romans 8:28-39 is such a passage. It is riddled with forensic imagery and ends with the apostle playing the role of a defense attorney, daring anyone in the courtroom to bring a charge against God or God's people:

> What shall we say to this?
> If God is for us, who is against us?
> He who did not spare his own Son
>   but gave him up for us all,
> will he not also give us all things with him?

Who shall bring any charge against God's elect?
It is God who justifies;
who is to condemn?
Is it Christ Jesus, who died,
    yes, who was raised from the dead? . . .

Who shall separate us from the love of Christ?
Shall tribulation, or distress, or persecution,
    or famine, or nakedness, or peril, or sword?

The Professor has slipped out of the building and a flamboyant southern lawyer has taken his place. How would you preach such a text? It seems to me, with a different style than the first two examples, one that reflects this passage's pacing, rhetorical questions, piling on of calamities, and evangelical defiance. You would preach it with a sense of *contest,* as if someone's life really depended on it.

Of course, any student of contemporary communication will tell you that the grand style is hopelessly out of date and will not work in this culture. It is not what people want to hear anymore. Paul is dead. Augustine is dead. All the great orators are dead. Passion is passé. You might remember this advice the next time you worship in one of the great African-American churches and find yourself weeping or clapping your hands or wanting to dance. Just tell yourself, "This isn't happening."

The preacher who is overly concerned with self-expression in the pulpit may be neglecting the rich array of styles available in the Bible. The *text* will tell you when to be angry, ironic, funny, or sad. It will tell you when to reason with your hearers and when to tease them with parabolic utterance, when to teach your parishioners in the synagogue and when to soar with them to the third heaven.

The Western heritage of preaching fixed a gulf between the *what* and the *how* of the sermon, and placed *how* in the subordinate position. As long as the preacher identified the correct doctrine in the passage it didn't matter what style he or she used to articulate it. But in the New Testament such words as "form," "likeness," and "image" *(morphê, schêma, eíkôn)* do not refer to external appearances only but to the entirety of the person or thing in question.[13] The shape of a tool defines the kind of work it will do, just as the form of a story or an argument is fundamental to how it will be preached.

For too long, however, preachers have imposed a few basic design schemes on any and every text. They have adopted only one formal approach to the sermon, and that based on the sole criterion of personal preference: "I am a three-point preacher." "I am a storyteller." "I only preach inductively." And, even more predictably, they have restricted their demeanor in the pulpit to the conventional persona of the religious lecturer.

13. Amos N. Wilder, *Early Christian Rhetoric* (Cambridge: Harvard University Press, 1964), p. 25.

Toward the beginning of the introductory preaching course, we invite students to perform a story from the Old Testament. Some students dance the text or sing it, others dramatize with complete abandon, and most succeed in losing themselves in the biblical text. The notion of *performance* in homiletics may provide much-needed relief from the tyranny of "my personal style." In its extended meanings, performance can refer to the manner in which the whole community embodies the biblical text. The community's interpretation of specific passages dealing with prayer, mission, or hospitality will not be written down but enacted in its daily existence. Bonhoeffer's community at Finkenwald, to cite a prominent example, performed the Scripture by ordering its entire life according to the rhythms of study and meditation on the word of God.

Similarly, the shape of an individual's witness may provide the ultimate interpretation of a biblical passage or concept. Oscar Romero's final sermon dealt with the church's Lenten journey through the valley of temptation, a concept whose interpretation he completed the next day by the shedding of his blood. Likewise, Bonhoeffer has been dubbed a performer of Scripture not because of any one sermon he preached but by the manner in which he lived and died. He made his definitive interpretation of discipleship long after he completed *The Cost of Discipleship.*

The concept of performance is so rich we must limit

ourselves to its more obvious meaning: A performer renders vocally an authoritative passage. The preacher does not merely talk about the text but crafts the sermon in such a way that it does what the text does. The sermon *joins* the text and participates in its witness to the church and world.

I am not suggesting that the preacher is obliged to create a sermon in the same genre as the text, for example, a parable-sermon on a parable or a blessing on a blessing, but only that the *spirit* of the genre be observed. As Fred Craddock suggested, let us not turn a beatitude into a strategy for attaining blessedness or a doxology into an analysis of the glory of God.[14]

The preacher performs texts much in the way an actor plays many parts or a musician renders different types of musical scores. If the only role Meryl Streep can play is Meryl Streep, she does not deserve accolades as an actor. But if she defers to the script and loses herself in the personality of her character, she is not only a great actor but a faithful performer, for she has discovered something in the script, winkled it out, and brought it alive. If we believe the Bible is performative, that it not only describes things but changes them, then preaching the Bible should do the same. P. T. Forsyth may have had the notion of performance on his mind (in 1907) when he

14. Fred B. Craddock, *Preaching* (Nashville: Abingdon, 1985), pp. 122-23.

claimed that the nearest analogue to the preacher is not the orator but the dramatist.[15]

The interpretation of the word begins with its voicing. The time and place of the reading as well as the mechanics of its intonation instantly suggest a meaning to the listener. When Ezra stood at the Water Gate and read the word, it was a way of announcing, "The Torah is back." When the members of the Open Door Community in Atlanta read the Scripture in a homeless shelter, a soup kitchen, or on the street, it is their way of saying, "God *belongs* in this place."

The preacher embodies the spirit of the text first in its reading and then more explicitly in its proclamation. Martin Luther King Jr., who according to one historian will be remembered as a daring dramatist of ideas, often performed the text of John 12:20-33, in which a delegation of Greeks comes to Philip and says, "Sir, we want to see Jesus." Many preachers might pass over the nationality of those who make this request as an incidental detail in the text. But in the Fourth Gospel the coming of the Gentiles signals the beginning of Christ's "hour" of fulfillment and is therefore of enormous significance in the narrative. King understands the fullness of the moment and therefore does not limit himself to a prosaic explanation of the relation of Greek culture to Hebrew religion or of the importance of "the hour" in the theology of John. Instead, he

15. P. T. Forsyth, *Positive Preaching and the Modern Mind* (Grand Rapids: Baker, 1980 [1907]), pp. 3-4.

celebrates the beauty of classical culture by savoring the names of its greatest representatives: *Aristophanes, Euripides, Thucydides, Demosthenes.* He does so in order to prepare his congregation for an even greater name. In the sermon "We Would See Jesus," he powerfully combines a profusion of Latinate sounds and classical names with a series of repetitions ending with the name "Jesus."

> "Sir, [they said] we would see Jesus, the light
>   of the world.
> We know about Plato, but we want to see Jesus.
> We know about Aristotle, but we want to see Jesus.
> We know about Homer, but we want to see Jesus."

His voice stabs at the first syllable of *Pla*-to and *Ho*-mer and drops at the end of each sentence to a gravelly and intimate *Jee*-sus. The voicing itself witnesses to the finality of Jesus in a world of high culture.[16] And all this because some Greeks said, "Sir, we want to see Jesus." The preacher is performing the text.

In a very different but no less performative mode, Rowan Williams plays on Peter's denial, "I do not know the man," implying that the word to be emphasized in that sentence is "man." Christians are oddly uncomfortable with the humanity of Christ. They do not wish to be im-

16. See Richard Lischer, *The Preacher King* (New York: Oxford, 1995), pp. 120-21.

84

plicated in the tawdriness of his arrest and suffering. Williams's passionate confession mirrors one of the most intense scenes in the New Testament:

> ### I do not know the man.
>
> I am more comfortable with the God. The man speaks to me not in solemn commands, in law and majesty, but the touch of a hand, a baby crying, a death, and expects me to hear and obey these voices of need and friendship as if they were the voice of God. . . .
>
> ### I do not know the man.
>
> I do not want to know the human, the provisional and ironic, tears and laughter, the future still to make. . . . Take us away from all this; like the ultimate romantic hero, sweep us into the world of distant panoramas, magical controls, solved problems. I do not want to be forced back to the earth where I must choose and travel and be hurt.
>
> ### I do not know the man.

What begins as Peter's dramatic liturgy of denial quickly shifts to that of every person in the church. Peter's cowardice is transformed into the profound confession of all imperfect disciples who, as the preacher says, "want the questions to stop."[17]

17. Rowan Williams, *A Ray of Darkness* (Cambridge, Mass.: Cowley, 1995), pp. 54-56.

Williams's reading is imaginatively true to the text. Though Peter himself does not confess his many fears, he and the other disciples are meant to stand for all believers, including us. We are all gathered around the fire and silently echo his words. Our failures of nerve represent the latest in a long series of denials suffered by Jesus.

Every preacher reads the text seeking that which is most powerfully *imitable* in it. Williams finds it in Everyman's fear and performs it with the dramatic intensity of the Passion narrative itself. In doing so, he reminds us that at its best preaching is a kind of leap of faith, an imaginative expansion into realms not easily discerned on the printed page.

We have come a long way from *How do you read?* which remains as challenging a question today as when Jesus first posed it. Implied in his question is the additional phrase, *given the lateness of the hour.* Under the pressure of God's claim upon our lives, symbolized by signs of the dawning kingdom, intimations of the end of history, and the certainty of our own death, how shall we read this Scripture in order to receive the blessing we do not deserve but desperately need?

In this chapter, we have moved *away* from the romantic notion of the loneliness of the preacher or individualistic exegesis. We no longer insist on *the* single, definitive meaning of any given passage. And we have uncoupled style from the preacher's personality and reconnected it to the readings and liturgy of the day.

We have moved *toward* a reading-strategy of trust in the faithfulness of God who is revealed in the text. In trust, we have come to embrace the possibility of multiple performances of biblical texts, each determined by the character of the passage and the needs of the community. In matters of interpretation, we have learned to listen with respect to voices other than our own.

We have begun to read the book as preachers, and unashamedly so, for we know the book was written to be proclaimed.

NARRATION

Chapter Three

One Last Story

*We crave nothing less than perfect story; and while
we chatter or listen all our lives in a din of craving —
jokes, anecdotes, novels, dreams, films, plays, songs,
half the words of our days — we are satisfied only by
the one short tale we feel to be true.*

Reynolds Price, *A Palpable God*

So far, we have explored what it means to have a vocation
in the word of God. The preacher's vocation entails a dying to the norms of those who control language in our
culture. It offers a resurrection of freedom to speak of
God in a God-free society and to join our words to the
suffering and joy of God's people. A vocation in the word
sends ripples of benefits to those who have forgotten that
they too have a sacred calling from God. Thus the preaching office is layered with responsibilities — to the truth of
the word itself, to one's own integrity as a speaker, to the
church, and to the world. No wonder Paul asked his con-

gregation in Ephesus to pray that he would preach the gospel as it ought to be done.

Having this vocation, how ought we to speak? In Chapter Two I suggested that the preacher has a peculiar method of answering that question. The preacher's sermon takes its spirit, style, and purpose from the biblical text. Instead of taking the analytical step back from the text, the preacher leaps into the text, goes deep, and surfaces on some other shore. What the preacher comes up with is not so much a new meaning but a new performance of the text, one that will enable its listeners to perform it themselves in their daily lives.

Thus at the center of our calling lies an imaginative act of reading that culminates in a public performance of what has been read. Augustine's word for the latter phase of this task was "style," for which he drew many of his examples from Paul and most of his inspiration from Cicero. For the past thirty years, however, American homiletics has shown little interest in Paul or Cicero. It has focused its attention almost exclusively on narrative as the most appropriate rhetorical form for the sermon.

From Code to Narrative

I have an old college friend I see so infrequently that when we get together we don't have time for lengthy reminiscences. The night wears on too quickly, and we have too much ground to cover. So we just throw out codes. The codes stand for the experiences and history we share. "Kilbourn Hall," he says. "Marvin's new luggage," I reply, and we collapse in paroxysms of joy as our families, who have heard it all before, drift off to bed. The codes still work for some to evoke rich memories and to seal relationships. But they also have the power to exclude and to turn family members into outsiders.

There was a time when preachers might have dispensed with the Bible's stories and tossed out codes such as "covenant," "providence," "salvation," or "discipleship," and those passwords would have called up a world of meaning for the listener. But the codes are working less effectively than ever before. To most people the word "covenant," for example, does not trigger the fabulous story of the promise to Abraham or the tragedy of beautiful King David or even the gracious sealing of the law at Sinai. Aside from the world of real estate law, the word appears to denote almost nothing. Recently, the school where I teach introduced a "covenant" by which to guide the academic and communal behavior of students and faculty. The rest of the university was perplexed, to the say the least, by a concept with which it could not reckon.

A generation ago theologians thought to solve the problem by translating the biblical codes into other codes, those drawn from psychotherapy, politics, or philosophy. The problem was that the secular codes only led us deeper into a thicket of additional terms and concepts that quickly became outdated and alien to ordinary people. But the more serious problem with the translation project was that it distanced theology from its own narrative framework and therefore from its own identity.

The literary critic Erich Auerbach contrasted the Old Testament with Homer by saying the former was "fraught with background." Homer's characters never change. Odysseus returns to Ithaca the very same person he was when he left twenty years before. The biblical Jacob, on the other hand, is tempered by suffering and regret. The pitiful old man grieving for his lost son is a different person from the trickster who cheated his brother out of his inheritance. The "background" of the story is precisely the dimension that has gone missing in contemporary preaching, which in many instances appears two-dimensional, restricted to an intensely personal relationship between God and the individual. The necessary background can be recovered only if preaching rediscovers its true narrative framework in Scripture and tradition.

But this is not easy. The audience may have little knowledge of the codes but even less time for the stories. By its nature, storytelling is a leisurely activity. It requires time for absorption — narrative *is* time arranged in language. I am convinced that one of the reasons the church continues to thrive in the South is that southerners have not lost the capacity to tell or hear a good story. I have friends who are constitutionally incapable of speaking in any mode other than narrative. If you ask them for the time, they will tell how they acquired the watch. To any factual question they can only reply, "That reminds me of a story."

The digital generation, however, has developed a bottom-line impatience with narrative. It doesn't take a literary critic to notice that real life in our culture moves at a faster pace than the Bible's stories about real life. Ours is a generation that will have a terrible time sitting still long enough to listen to messages that begin, as does 1 Samuel, "There was a certain man of Ramathaim-zophim of the hill country of Ephraim, whose name was Elkanah the son of Jeroham, son of Elihu, son of Tohu, son of Zuph, an Ephraimite." This is a beautiful Hebrew sentence that meanders like a brook, but the contemporary hearer is already listening for the punch line or the payoff. "What does this have to do with me?" Like the cycle of narratives it introduces, 1 Samuel 1:1 poses a serious challenge to the time-kept preacher.

Fortunately, the church has many forms of speech, including the language of immediacy and personal involvement. Before we turn our attention to narrative, let me put in a word for decisive speech, for language that sunders the teller from the artifice of the tale. (Remember, the narrator is a character in the narration.) The preacher must retain the capacity to lower the narrator's mask and to tell the truth directly and decisively from a pastoral heart.

What is decisive speech? Decisive speech is language

that claims your attention and with it your will. It invades
your space, takes your face in its hands, and demands to be
heard. It is not afraid to say "you." There may be indirect
ways of expressing one's love, but there is no substitute for
saying the words. There may be narrative techniques for
suggesting, "Your sins are forgiven" or "Go in peace, serve
the Lord," but there is no substitute for the joyous an-
nouncement. The angel's gospel "He is risen!" is not a story
but a status-report of the way things are with God and you
and the universe — now. If you enter a medical consulting
room facing a potentially serious diagnosis, the last thing
you want to hear is the history of the disease, the evolution
of its treatment, or a couple anecdotes about the doctor's
brother-in-law who may or may not have had a similar
malady. You want to know where you stand — now.

Fortunately, the church has been given a language
that allows us to speak with the angels. Such language
does not first evoke a situation and try to correlate divine
revelation with it. It simply drops words like "redemption," "hope," or "eternal life" into unredeemed, hopeless,
terminal situations and allows the word to do the work.
This sort of decisive speech is often associated with the
preaching of Karl Barth, whose sermons to the prisoners
in the Basel jail do not evoke the specificities of prison
life but are unmistakably addressed to those in captivity.[1]

1. See Karl Barth, *Deliverance to the Captives,* trans. Marguerite
Wiser (Westport, Conn.: Greenwood, 1979).

Both decisive speech and narrative abound in Scripture, and both permeate our everyday experience. We know there are times in our lives, namely, every day, when we need a word spoken directly to us from the heart as simple as "I love you" or "This gift is for you" or "This you must do." But we also know there are other times, namely, every day, when we lean across the desk or lunch table, our senses expectant, because someone has just said to us, "Let me tell you a story."

The Ways of Story

As a new pastor in a congregation, I was always surprised by how often on my first visit with parishioners they would tell me the story of the worst thing that had ever happened to them. By parting the curtain on their past, they seemed to be opening a door to our future relationship. They would have agreed with storyteller Karen Blixen, who said, "Any sorrow can be borne if a story can be told about it." Any good story with a beginning, a middle, and an end creates its own order and with it its own natural hope. It is as if the narrative form itself is offering to both narrator and reader an imaginative means of survival.

The journey from beginning through middle to end in any story is called a plot. One critic compares plot to a broom that sweeps in one direction. It imposes a sense of direction and purpose on any combination of events. Every text, including the epistles in the New Testament as well as the subtlest progressions of Hebrew poetry in the Old Testament, contains some incremental movement or rudimentary story line that would qualify as a plot.

Every sermon should have a plot as well, which is a purpose that cannot be stated all at once but must unfold toward a destination, the way Jesus' ministry *moved* episodically toward the cross or the way God's love unfolds day by day in our lives. Perhaps what my parishioners were looking for in the stories they told me was a plot. For in a plot things happen in some logical order and to some meaningful end. Despite our culture's growing impatience with complex biblical narratives, we are all characters in search of a plot. And we hope our little plots will link up to others in a larger and more comprehensive narrative.

At the very suggestion of a larger framework, postmodernism throws up its hands and denounces all master stories. "No more grand narratives," it pleads. The world has paid a terrible price for totalizing discourse, which imposes the stencil of one story on many peoples and cultures. Ask the Jews about the Grand Narrative. Ask the Native Americans, African Americans, immigrants, the women, all of whom were forcibly assigned roles in other people's stories.

It would be another chapter to explore the grand narratives that have shaped modern life: how the Enlighten-

ment cast the history of humanity as the story of the pro-
gressive attainment of reason; how Darwin implicated
humankind in the history of nature; how Marx exposed
capitalism's history of exploitation; how Freud re-
narrated us as characters in our own myth, the Oedipal.
Modernity spawned the master stories with which we are
all familiar: freedom versus tyranny, the survival of the
fittest, evolutionary progress, manifest destiny, the joy of
self-discovery.

After the fall of the Soviet Union, a former State De-
partment analyst, Francis Fukuyama, wrote a best-seller
called *The End of History.* With the cessation of conflict
between East and West, he argued, Hegel's dream of universal history has been realized. Liberal democracy represents the final stage of the dialectic beyond which there
is nothing more and nothing better. Thus we have
reached the end of history. The end is characterized by a
catholicity of technology, which, says Fukuyama, "makes
possible the limitless accumulation of wealth, and thus
the satisfaction of an ever-expanding set of human de-
sires." In the absence of difference, want, and conflict, history comes to an end.[2]

Who is to say he is wrong or that history has some
other purpose? Who is to say that the immense power
that controls not only the armies of the world but also

2. Francis Fukuyama, *The End of History and the Last Man* (New
York: Free Press, 1992), pp. xiv-xv.

the discourses of the world will not create one brave new world in which anything is technically and therefore morally possible? Who is to say that some "rough beast," as the poet Yeats imagined it in "The Second Coming," is not even now slouching toward New York with a few surprises? Who is to say that some shadowy monster or shining hero does not hold the spinal cord of history in his hands?

Who is to say? Why, the preacher, who else? Not one lonely preacher, of course, but the whole company of preachers stretching as far as the eye can see, and beyond them to all those who have the courage to narrate another history.

Early narrative preaching tended to celebrate what it called the narrativity of human experience. One narrative theologian reminded us that we think, dream, daydream, remember, doubt, hope, and organize our lives in narrative.[3] The narrative form is congenial to the natural rhythms of our lives. Narrative homileticians focused on the goodness of story without adequately examining the sort of story we tell and the nature of its competition with other stories.

But "simple" storytelling turned out to be a misnomer.

---

3. Brian Wicker, *The Story-Shaped World* (Notre Dame, Ind.: University of Notre Dame Press, 1975), p. 47 cited in Fred B. Craddock, *Overhearing the Gospel* (Nashville: Abingdon, 1978), p. 139. The relevant section is reproduced in *The Company of Preachers,* ed. Richard Lischer (Grand Rapids: Eerdmans, 2002), pp. 401-8.

Storytelling is a battle. For Christians are living waist-deep in competing narratives — stories of empire, nation, progress, and self-actualization, each of which whispers in our ear, "This is who you really are. You belong to us."

If you've ever told a child a bedtime story, you know that what you actually tell is a *series* of stories, usually in the same order. And as you begin to wind down as a storyteller, the child invariably asks, "Just one last story," knowing that the last story will be the true story and the one that will secure her place in the narrative.

I think of the preacher as the one who tells the world's last story. But what is its nature?

Christians are often accused of purveying a Grand Narrative whose only function has been to dominate the narrative aspirations of other religions and worldviews. Any story that purports to explain everything about human life from creation to consummation must eventually prove to be a tool of oppression, or so goes the argument. Three features of the Christian story, however, differentiate it from the Grand Narratives of modernity, and all three are related to preaching.

The first is the perspectival character of its telling. Our story is narrated by a fallible witness called a "preacher," on the basis of smallish and sometimes ambiguous stories called "texts," amidst a less-than-powerful minority group called a "congregation." That it identifies itself as a witness or a confession testifies to its vulnerability in a world of totalizing discourse.

The second factor is the cross. The Christian story pivots on the execution of a teacher who claimed to be the Messiah. Why God would choose such a lowly instrument of redemption is inexplicable even to Christian believers. According to Luther, the theology of the cross protects us from total knowledge of God. When we preach from that jagged perspective, the empowerment we receive comes at the expense of a triumphal mastery of life.

The third and final factor is this, that our story, no matter how grand and comprehensive its scope, remains unfinished.[4] Only God knows how it will all turn out. At this point on our pilgrimage, therefore, we can make no claims to total knowledge. Every sermon based on this story has about it a promissory quality. Most Grand Narratives do not confess, "For now we see through a glass darkly. . . ."

Christians tell their story self-critically in full recognition of their susceptibility to the pervasive power of other stories. The preacher helps us discern how the world's stories have captivated us all: How we are all children of a greedy economic system. How we are all worshipers of the self. How we are all slaves to the great god success. Then the preacher gently and patiently teases apart the skein of these familiar narratives from "the last story,"

4. Gerard Loughlin, *Telling God's Story* (Cambridge: Cambridge University Press, 1996), p. 24.

which among all the plots and subplots of the world is uniquely redemptive. The separating of stories is a delicate theological procedure because the accounts of self, nation, and success encircle vital organs. This is perhaps why one of the most enduring metaphors for the preacher, used by both Jonathan Edwards and Martin Luther King, is the surgeon.

The purpose of separating the stories is not to condemn the world's stories or to replace them with a more attractive story. The gospel takes the stories of this age seriously. If we are to find redemption it will be in the midst of the many stories we are living out in this world. We cannot shed our culturally inscribed attributes the way a snake sheds its skin. Contemporary Christians are imbued with a sense of self that our forefathers and foremothers knew nothing about. We accept technology, mass communications, and medical science as psychospatial extensions of our human nature. Like many others in the West, we have benefited from the Enlightenment quest for personal and political freedom. Not many of us would want to live in a world that was never home to Thomas Jefferson and did not include the narrative of inalienable human rights.

The familiar myths of modernity were once the challengers to the divinely revealed story of salvation. They conspired to replace God's agency in the world with human achievement. Now they rule. Their success created scientific and political breakthroughs, but it also helped fashion a world in which God, the cross, and salvation have been restricted to personal opinion or relegated to the margins of human society. In the wake of modernity, it is faithful disciples and ordinary preachers who have become the counter-narrativists, the rebels, who now dare to tell the world another, more excellent story.

The Art of Preaching

Every day, Christians are sorting through their narrative options and claiming an identity as followers of Jesus Christ. On Sunday, the preacher helps them in this task by means of a poetic activity. The preacher makes *(poiein)* words, approximately fifteen hundred of them on a Sunday morning, three million in a career, and over the long haul of ministry, he or she speaks into existence an alternative world. Theologian John Snow says the pastoral counselor helps fashion a world in which Christian symbols make sense.[5] This is also true of the preacher, who Sunday by Sunday patiently and often unspectacularly crafts a world in which the personages, events, and radical claims of the gospel ring true, a world in which the risen Christ is a genuine factor in the daily lives of his followers. The sermon's narrative runs

5. John H. Snow, *The Impossible Vocation* (Cambridge, Mass.: Cowley, 1988), p. 53.

continuously like the old serial matinees at the movies, but the preacher experiences the sermon as an artistic and religious endeavor that must be repeated every week.

Generations ago, G. K. Chesterton was promoting the gospel to an industrial age that conceived of the world as a self-sustaining machine. In a delightful passage from his book *Orthodoxy* Chesterton insists that even if life does proceed with a predictable pattern, that does not mean that God is not active as a creator. He says,

> [I]t might be true that the sun rises regularly because he never gets tired of rising. His routine might be due, not to a lifelessness, but to a rush of life. The thing I mean can be seen . . . in children, when they find some game or joke that they specially enjoy. A child kicks his legs rhythmically through excess, not absence, of life. Because children have abounding vitality, because they are in spirit fierce and free, therefore they want things repeated and unchanged. They always say, "Do it again"; and the grown-up person does it again until he is nearly dead. For grown-up people are not strong enough to exult in monotony. But perhaps God is strong enough to exult in monotony. It is possible that God says every morning, "Do it again" to the sun; and every evening, "Do it again" to the moon. It may not be automatic necessity that makes all daisies alike; it may be that God makes every daisy separately, but has

never got tired of making them. It may be that He has the eternal appetite of infancy.[6]

Preaching is one of God's "do it again" activities. The sermon is a repetitive practice that has changed little in twenty-one centuries, but it is also a new creation that no one could produce on a weekly basis were it not for the Almighty's "eternal appetite of infancy."

When the adopted child repeatedly asks her parents to recount the events surrounding her adoption, the story must remain the same. And woe to the one who introduces omissions or changes in the sacred formula. *"And then of all the babies in the orphanage, you chose me, right?"*

Could parents ever tire of telling that story? Would they ever dare substitute another for it? If telling God's story strikes us as repetitious, that is because it is. It is repetitious the way the Eucharist is repetitious, the way a favorite melody or gestures of love are repetitious, the way the mercies of God that come unbidden every day are repetitious.

When the community gathers around its table, one of its representatives narrates a particular story, either of deliverance from Egypt or of a Passover meal laden with the solemn promise of a new covenant. The community does not substitute a new formula or a better story for

6. Gilbert K. Chesterton, *Orthodoxy* (New York: Doubleday, 1990 [1908]), p. 60.

the sake of innovation but recites *this* story as faithfully as possible. "Then of all the peoples on earth," say the Jews every Sabbath, "you chose us, right?"

Such stories do not entertain, they do something far better. They *sustain*. They do not inform, they *form* those who hear and share them for a life of faithfulness.

Preaching participates in this age-old chain of repetition, sustenance, and formation. How is it then that we claim the sermon as a work of art, given the unoriginality of its basic components and the conventionality of its expression? If one's notion of art is limited to what is new, preaching the old story is not art. If the idea of art is restricted to poetic self-expression, then preaching the church's gospel in public does not qualify. If "art" means inspirational stories and pretty metaphors, there is so much in the Bible that is neither inspirational nor pretty that biblical preaching, at least, will probably not be mistaken for art.

But if your idea of art is something the creature, who knows she is a creature, sings back to the Creator with something of the Creator's own pizzazz (as Annie Dillard put it), then preaching has the potential, at least, to be more like art and less like an endowed lecture series. The preacher makes a small, shaped offering of truth back to the Truth itself. If you think of art as part discipline, part craft, and part mystery, we may be on to something.

For the Presbyterian minister in Norman Maclean's *A River Runs through It*, preaching the gospel is something like another highly repetitive activity, fly fishing. Both entail elements of art, beauty, patience, and mystery. The narrator remembers, "My father was very sure about certain matters pertaining to the universe. To him, all good things — trout as well as eternal salvation — come by grace and grace comes by art and art does not come easy."[7]

Grace comes by art and art does not come easy because God is not clumsy. God never blunders onto the scene with obviousness but is always draped by a story, an ordinary experience, or a metaphor. As Barth says, "God is so unassuming in the world."[8]

Many preachers, however, tell stories (note the plural) as if they served the purpose of making the Bible more interesting. Preachers have a sixth sense for what makes for a good story. A good story is touching, funny, marked by conflict (but not too much conflict), and satisfying in its resolution. Some preachers then repackage the gospel into stories that satisfy these criteria. Sermon stories "illustrate" the truth or substitute for those dusty old tales in the Bible that no one understands anyway.

Sermon illustrations often live a life separate from the theological truth they are meant to illumine. They enjoy a

7. Norman Maclean, *A River Runs through It* (New York: Pocket Books, 1992 [1976]), p. 5.

8. Karl Barth, *Church Dogmatics,* trans. G. W. Bromiley, vol. 4, pt. 2 (Edinburgh: T. & T. Clark, 1958), p. 291. The sentence continues, "but so revolutionary in relation to it. . . ."

timeless and disembodied existence on the Internet, where we encounter them as fileable nuggets of other people's experience. You can borrow or buy other preachers' illustrations without even bothering with text, context, or personal involvement in the hard work of discovery. The stories are usually about famous people or the enduring stuff of universal experience, but they cannot satisfy the congregation's deepest longing, which is to explore its own life before God in as concrete a fashion as possible.

As everyone knows but few admit, the tacit purpose of sermon illustrations is emotional gratification — pleasure. Since Aristotle, we've known there is something pleasurable about *mimesis,* the imitation of life as it is portrayed in drama, literature, and even sermons, especially when the mimetic activity accurately portrays our most cherished or fearful experiences. Its pleasure is enhanced when the illustration is skillfully yoked to a familiar theme and yields an easily digested moral lesson.

That story performs this function is a judgment not on *mimesis* or pleasure in itself, but on our understanding of the gospel as inherently abstract when, as Bonhoeffer reminds us, the most concrete of all realities is that of the person before the cross.[9]

Some narrative preachers treat the gospel as though

9. Bonhoeffer, *Worldly Preaching,* trans. Clyde E. Fant (New York: Thomas Nelson, 1975), p. 142.

it were one of several species under the genus "story," when in fact the Bible's narrative of salvation sets the standard for what a story should be. Only by light of the gospel do we discover our true beginning, middle, and end.

How far we preachers have traveled from the true ground of narrative preaching. We tell *stories* by reason of our humanity. In the pulpit, however, preachers tell *the* story because God got involved with a particular people in a specific time and place, and that involvement generated a history in which we are privileged to participate by faith, baptism, and the common life. We are not generic storytellers. We are nailed to a particular plot. The preacher's task is not to tell bunches of substitute stories, which in the end only deflect our attention from the searing reality of the person before God, but to tell that one story, the one that precedes the general category of "story," and to tell it in such a way that it makes our stories permeable to it.

Narrative Alternatives

My alternative to the sermon illustration, which tends to take over the sermon and detract from the gospel, is what Robert Tannehill in another context called "the focal instance." He was speaking of the skill with which the narrators of the Gospels package their theology of Jesus in vivid and "extreme" scenarios, which are specific slices of life with larger and wider implications.[10] In the Sermon on the Mount, for example, Jesus is teaching the importance of reconciliation when he says, "So when you are offering your gift at the altar, if you remember that your brother or sister has something against you, leave your gift there before the altar and go; first be reconciled to your brother or sister, and then come and offer your gift" (Matt. 5:23-24). He has provided a visual instance of his teaching on reconciliation without overwhelming it with a ponderous story. The focal instance makes the gospel real for the reader, but it never overshadows or moralizes it. The focal instance in the sermon functions somewhat like the saints, who are vivid, interesting human beings, but only *saints* because they steadfastly refuse to be anything more than models of their Original. The saints never preen or call attention to themselves. The focal instance means to say, in effect, "This is the message of God's grace; and this is what that grace looks like when it intersects the lives of real people. See?"

Among modern preachers one thinks of the power of *scene* in Frederick Buechner or Barbara Brown Taylor's ability to illumine the gospel in prototypal human situations. In her sermon "He Who Fills All in All" Taylor skillfully contrasts the failures of the institutional church

10. Robert C. Tannehill, *The Sword of His Mouth* (Philadelphia: Fortress, 1975), pp. 67-77.

with the faithful lives of its members, citing as an instance an unnamed woman who, though dying of cancer and burdened with an oxygen tank slung over her shoulder, reads the lesson for Christmas Eve in her local congregation.

> Her tank hisses every five seconds. Every candle in the place glitters in her eyes. "Strengthen the weak hands," she reads, bending her body toward the words, "and make firm the feeble knees. Say to those who are of a fearful heart, 'Be strong, do not fear! Here is your God.'" When she sits down, the congregation knows they have not just *heard* the word of the Lord. They have seen it in action.[11]

Taylor's focal instance works nicely, especially in relation to a text that focuses on *seeing* the grace of God — "having the eyes of your heart enlightened, that you may know what is the hope to which he has called you" (Eph. 1:18).

There are many ways a narrative preacher might have ruined this sermon! One way would have been to impose a story line on the focal instance, relating too many invasive details of the woman's life and subsequent fate. An-

---

11. Barbara Brown Taylor, *Home by Another Way* (Cambridge, Mass.: Cowley, 1999), p. 140. The video version of her sermon is titled "God's Ruined Church."

other way of reducing the impact of the focal instance might have been the preacher's own intrusive presence in the sermon, which could have only deflected the listener's attention from the woman in the story to the preacher's relationship with the woman. A third way to ruin an instance of grace might have occurred if the preacher had added a moral or a practical lesson to the story, which would have emptied the scene of its magic and robbed it of its epiphany-like character. Taylor does not make these mistakes, and therefore for a moment, at least, the hearer *sees* with the eyes of his heart.

A second narrative technique also follows the example of the New Testament. It tells a little story about Jesus. The four Gospels contain micro-plots of God's history with Israel and the church, each of which artfully encapsulates the meaning of Christ's death and resurrection. Each story offers a slant of light into a world haunted by Christ's presence. Each story has a few loose ends, but each concludes with what one literary critic calls "the same Single Surprise."[12]

The New Testament tells these little stories sermonically in order to render a clearer or more provocative portrait of Jesus. Contemporary preachers should render them as well, but in a different register and a new idiom. One of the problems with narrative preaching is the mind-

12. Hortense J. Spillers, *Black, White, and in Color* (Chicago: University of Chicago Press, 2003), p. 263.

numbing duplication with which it retells the biblical story in its original idiom. What gives the biblical story its edge is its capacity for being told by someone embedded in a different time and place who doesn't have to pretend to be a first-century fisherman. The point of narrative preaching is not to reconstruct the past but to celebrate what is alive in it and play it forward in ever-changing settings.

When it came to telling these little stories about Jesus, there was no finer narrative preacher than Martin Luther. What made Luther an effective narrative preacher was the German earthiness with which he performed the Bible's stories. When he tells of the nativity, for example, you can hear the carousers up the hill in the inn swilling their beer and singing their bawdy songs while a scared teenager named Maria is having her first baby alone in the dark, without so much as a candle or heated water. Now, the last time I checked, these details were not in the Bible! Luther adds imaginative coloring not to make the biblical account a "better" story but to allow the story to be itself in the world.

Luther would have seconded P. T. Forsyth's axiom that the cure for pulpit dullness is not brilliance but reality.[13] The antidote to the air of unreality that hangs like a canopy over so many pulpits will be found in the Bible's steely realism about God and human nature.

13. P. T. Forsyth, *Positive Preaching and the Modern Mind* (Grand Rapids: Baker, 1980 [1907]), p. 91.

A man brings Jesus to his boy who is writhing in the throes of a terrifying seizure. Jesus looks at the boy and launches into a sermon, "All things are possible to those who believe." And the man, who is apparently in no mood for a sermon, interrupts him with the reply, "Lord, I believe. Help my unbelief." If the preacher can tell that story and not be riveted by the same ambiguity, the evangelist has written in vain.

In the parables of Jesus, to cite another example of the Bible's realism, one encounters the reality of God in the ordinary lives of *petite bourgeois* Palestinians. The supernatural is about as visible in the parables as it is in our world. The parables of Jesus offer no easy answers or a *deus ex machina.* Aristotle might have been referring to them when he said in the *Poetics* that good drama need not describe "the thing that has happened but the kind of thing that *might* happen." Not photographic or invasive, he would have said today, but suggestive or inclusive.

Classicist Erich Auerbach does not find in all Greco-Roman literature a story comparable to Peter's encounter with the servant girl in the high priest's courtyard. Peter is the leader of the Christian movement, and yet the literature of the movement implicates him in a tawdry deception with dialogue so realistic that it's embarrassing. In classical literature, underlings like the servant girl appear, of course, but only in comic situations. Poor people were not capable of tragedy. But thanks to the Gospels' theological realism, readers of ordinary Greek *koine* could identify with similar scenarios in their own lives. As we watch that scene unfold by the crackling fire, we recall the ways we ourselves have insisted, "I tell you, I do not know the man," and something in us is cleansed. "It was the story of Christ," Auerbach concludes in *Mimesis,* "with its ruthless mixture of everyday reality and the highest and most sublime tragedy, which had conquered the classical rule of styles."[14]

The source of the New Testament's realism is the cross. There is an ugly incident at Golgotha that mars the landscape of contemporary storytelling and popular spirituality. Let me complete the earlier allusion to John Snow's book *The Impossible Vocation:* "If [preaching] is the construction of a world in which Christian symbols make sense, there must be room in this world for loss and the opportunity for loss to be addressed by these symbols, by the metaphorical theological language of the church."[15]

From a similar perspective the sociologist Arthur Frank criticizes modern medical literature for its predilection for the happy ending or what Frank calls the "restitution narrative." In the restitution narrative medical science solves every problem and fixes everything that is broken. In his own illness Frank confronted what he calls

---

14. Erich Auerbach, *Mimesis,* trans. Willard Trask (Garden City, N.Y.: Doubleday-Anchor, 1953), p. 490. On tragedy, see p. 37.

15. Snow, *The Impossible Vocation,* p. 53.

the chaos narrative in which nothing gets fixed and the individual experiences disorientation to every conceivable horizon of meaning.[16]

At the epicenter of the gospel we encounter God's own chaos narrative summarized in Paul's phrase, the "word of the cross" (1 Cor. 1:18). As a preacher, Paul worried that too much eloquence — we might say, too many good stories — would detract from his message and rob the divine chaos of its power (1 Cor. 1:17). To the evangelists and Paul, the chaos does not represent a sidebar or a footnote to the main story. For an awful moment it rules, as in Jesus' cry of dereliction, "My God, my God, why have you forsaken me?" Each story in the Gospels artfully portrays someone's battle with the very same forces of dissolution. It was chaos in the fishing boat on the Sea of Galilee. It was chaos when the little boy was having convulsions at the feet of Jesus. It was chaos in Gethsemane when "his sweat became like great drops of blood."

It is important to let people know that God has taken up the "narrative wreckage" of our lives into God's own history, because many people think of the Christian story as a simple restitution narrative. They send money to preachers who promise to fix everything that is broken, from salvation to self-esteem.

16. Arthur W. Frank, *The Wounded Storyteller* (Chicago: University of Chicago Press, 1995), pp. 75-114.

The New Testament itself is a collection of unresolved and sometimes chaotic episodes whose plot can be completed only by those who hear and retell them. "Go, tell your friends what great things God has done for you," Jesus says. We never see them do that, for it is clear that we, the readers, are meant to perform the rest of the story. Against a backdrop of persecution, the curtain falls on the New Testament with a sigh of longing for something not yet consummated: "Even so, come, Lord Jesus."

There is a rhetoric of preaching, however, that treats unfinished stories, chaotic reversals, and apocalyptic sighs with such practiced symmetry that it vitiates the unfinished quality of the narratives. There is a homiletics so obsessed with form, or what rhetoric called *arrangement* — points, steps, blocks, moves, illustrations — that it loses touch with the New Testament's rhetoric, which is characterized by astonishment and self-abandonment to God's future. Science and sociology have ably informed us of the laws and trends that will keep us unwell, unhappy, and unrich. They have told us what we will *not* do under any circumstances. Let the preacher tell us what we might become if we live into this story.

So far, I have suggested two modes of narrative preaching: the *focal instance* and the *perspectival retelling of the biblical story*. With both suggestions came a plea to observe the New Testament's methods of telling stories about Jesus. The final narrative technique is more challenging.

The illustrations in most sermons are dispensable. That is to say, you can leave a few out, and the sermon will not be destroyed; in fact, it may even prosper. The final narrative technique employs a master metaphor whose elaboration defines and controls the entire sermon. Unlike the illustration, the metaphor is *not* dispensable but essential to the sermon, for in a mysterious way metaphor encompasses the apparent contradiction of specific instances and abstract ideas. An illustration confirms to its hearers something they already know. A metaphor discloses a reality that at some level the hearer has not imagined.

When it is young, a metaphor produces a shock to the sensibilities. According to Aristotle, metaphor always whispers, "It is/It is not." Once upon a time, Jesus' words "I am the Good Shepherd" must have produced a metaphoric shock among their first readers or hearers, since in the Old Testament it is *God* who promises to shepherd the people of Israel. Christians are still nurtured by this master metaphor, but the original shock has given way to feelings of comfort and assurance. Thirty years ago the musical *Godspel* produced a low-voltage shock when it presented Jesus not as a shepherd but as a clown. The initial reaction of many was, "It is not" and then, only grudgingly, "It might be."

Paul Tillich has a sermon on the burial of Jesus titled "Born in the Grave." After reading the account of Jesus' burial, the preacher tells the story of a man who during the Second World War fled a concentration camp near Wilna, Poland, and was forced to live in a Jewish cemetery. One day, he noticed a young woman in the grave next to his giving birth to a baby. In her delivery she was assisted by an old man dressed in a shroud. When the newborn uttered its first cries, the old man lifted the baby to heaven and said, "Great God, hast thou sent us Messiah? For who but Messiah could be born in a grave?"[17]

As with any metaphor, there is much that is "wrong" with this story, not the least of which is the repellent association of new life with the place of death. Babies are born in hospitals, not graves, and nurses wear crisp white uniforms and not shrouds. Moreover, if the preacher feels the need to introduce the parable by saying, "This story teaches us that Jesus had to be really dead and buried so that God's glory could be manifested in the resurrection," the metaphoric shock is reduced and the process of discovery is subverted, the way explaining a joke ruins it. Remove this metaphor from Tillich's sermon, and the whole sermon falls to pieces.

In his sermon "My Dancing Day," Rowan Williams provides another example of a metaphoric narrative. The preacher tells of watching a Chilean dance teacher who specializes in teaching mentally handicapped people

---

17. Paul Tillich, *The Shaking of the Foundations* (New York: Scribner's, 1948), p. 165, paraphrased.

how to dance. The teacher masterfully guides even the most awkward of her pupils around the floor, leading but not dominating, always allowing her partners just enough freedom to try their wings on the dance floor.

But *put* grace and you will *find* grace. Invite the un-lovely partner to sit opposite you, breathing slowly and deeply, and to mirror your gestures: the slow circling of an arm, the opening of a hand. That's how our Chilean teacher began. That's how dancing begins. . . . I'll give you grace and you can give it back. You can answer me because you are like me. You are alive, too. Here are the signs of my life, the patterns I make, the beauty I create, and so can you.

Soon it is clear that we are all "handicapped, lumpish, empty, afraid" and that none of us is so self-assured that we do not need this special partner. For "he knows he is lovely and loved. Dancing is natural to him. . . . So he be-gins: he stretches out his arms, wide as he can. And so do you. . . ."

He dances so that you will dance. He shows you what beauty is, his body awakens yours. He's there to be your partner and everyone's; sometimes you'll see him op-posite you, sometimes not (beside you, behind you, holding someone else's hands). But he's there, in and out of your dance, always affirming your beauty, fusing together your mind and your imagination and your flesh, so that none of it will be lost.[18]

Williams's sermon achieves a gorgeous articulation of the gospel by voicing it in a new key. Of course, the preacher already has a relationship-metaphor at his disposal, namely, the image of the shepherd, but he chooses a less familiar one. The dance itself is not a new metaphor for the believer's relationship with Jesus, but the sort of dance Williams evokes is not only fresh but revelatory. The sermon is as graceful as the dance it describes. There is nothing mechanical about the sermon. It does not illustrate, explain, or apply truths; nor does it deploy the beauty of its style in a way that calls attention to itself. The preacher lets his metaphor do all the work. He does not use the sermon's form as an excuse for sloppy thinking, artsy language, or unclarity. No one could have left church that day wondering who the preacher was talking about or if the sermon had given voice to the gospel. Such is the power of the Holy Spirit, the imagination, and the third narrative mode, the elaboration of a master metaphor in the sermon.

18. Rowan Williams, *A Ray of Darkness* (Cambridge, Mass.: Cowley, 1995), pp. 61-63.

One Last Story

But Is It True?

Throughout these comments on narrative I have assumed that there is such a thing as *the* Christian story. As everyone knows, this is a disputed claim. Under the centrifugal pressure of postmodernism (with the center not holding), many scholars deny the essential identity of Christianity and focus instead on the diversity of its traditions. And who would deny that Christianity has taken as many forms as there are communities and as many agendas as there are interested parties? Upon close inspection, the so-called story of Jesus turns out to be stories about Jesus, differing from one another not only in detail but in theological theme as well. As one theologian says, "You need not deconstruct these texts. They fall apart in your hands."[19]

Instead of a master story whose one size fits all, the preacher works with the little narratives of Scripture that open onto a multitude of human situations and support a variety of readings. There is no way one can make a

19. William C. Placher, *Narratives of a Vulnerable God* (Louisville: Westminster/John Knox, 1994), p. 91. Placher is not attempting to deconstruct the Gospels or denigrate their trustworthiness any more than Luther was when he noticed that the Gospel texts "have a queer way of talking, like people who, instead of proceeding in an orderly manner, ramble off from one thing to the next, so that you cannot make head or tail of them or see what they are getting at" (quoted by Placher, p. 91).

Grand Narrative out of the parable of the Dishonest Steward or the story of the Strange Exorcist. You can't build a "Be-happy Church" on the story of Ananias and Sapphira. Such stories seem designed to block us from saying too much about God. But they also invite preachers to do what each of the stories does in its Gospel setting, namely, to open a small window on the community's life with God.

And yet, in our rush to accommodate postmodernism, we can easily overlook the theological and artistic coherence of the Gospels. They may not dominate as a single Grand Narrative, but they do hang together. It doesn't matter that their stories disagree with one another in detail or theme, or that they fail to satisfy the canons of scientific history. The preacher's question is, are they sufficiently thick, real, and life-giving to render a figure who *was* a historical person and *is* alive and loose in the world?

If you are meeting a stranger at the airport (and you have an aversion to holding up a little sign that says "Professor Jones"), you need a description of that person. You don't need a birth certificate or exhaustive documentation, but the description must be accurate enough to enable you to recognize Professor Jones when she arrives.

From its inception the church experienced Jesus as risen from the dead. It did so in memory, witness, worship, and in the breaking of bread. All it needed by way of narration was a recognizable, embraceable description of Jesus. The theologian Hans Frei and others have argued persuasively that the purpose of the Gospels was never to provide an exhaustive history but to make Polaroids of Jesus the church could hold up in a hospital, prison, ghetto, or cemetery, so that we would know him when we meet him.

When we make a family album we do not do so to prove the existence of our ancestors or to provide a record of their appearance. We do it for our children and grandchildren in order to make a meeting possible, to enlarge their sense of identity and place in a family of love. Which is precisely our purpose in narrative preaching — not to prove points about Jesus but to evoke the one who is always among us, but hidden.

The stories may fall apart in our hands, but the one they render does not. The stories of Jesus haunt our world not because they correspond perfectly to history or science but because they correspond to his real presence among us.

Often it is the poet or artist who most powerfully recognizes the correspondence. In his memoir *A Whole New Life,* one such artist, novelist Reynolds Price, tells of his battle with cancer and his meeting with Jesus by the Lake of Gennesaret, when at the dawn of the author's first day of radiation treatments, a taciturn Jesus leads him waist deep into the water, washes him, forgives him, and heals him. With that done, Price is seamlessly returned to his own bed in North Carolina. It is pointless to ask the typical modernist questions, "Did it happen? How did it happen?" Perhaps it is enough to admit that a man in trouble met a savior who was clearly recognizable from one of his pictures. In telling his story Price operates as a preacher, creating a little world that encompasses Galilee *and* North Carolina, a world in which the risen Christ is really present.

The cure for pulpit dullness is not brilliance but reality — albeit a much bigger reality than we imagined, bigger than history or psychology, so big that it transfigures everything we so confidently named "reality."

Preachers are forever wringing their hands over the fragility of Christianity. Won't the gospel be crushed to smithereens by Communism, evolution, Islam, or secularism? we ask. But artists like Price testify to the resilience of the story and its power to replenish the human spirit. If we listen to the artists, they seem to be saying to the preachers, "You have the greatest story in the world. Trust your material."

Several years ago when Hurricane Fran hit the North Carolina coast and then, inexplicably, made a hard left turn and came inland to our city, it destroyed countless homes, uprooted thousands of trees, and in a few minutes changed the face of our community. On Sunday morning our congregation gathered in its darkened sanctuary still without power and light. We were a devastated group of people. Our pastor had the good sense to preface the liturgy by inviting anyone who wished to do so to tell a hurricane story. Lutherans do not do this. But after an appropriate display of reticence, we began. Some witnesses recounted rather trivial losses, like an air conditioner or a favorite tree, but others were terrible. It soon became clear, however, that we had more than a hurricane on our minds. A woman testified of a cancer she had endured, another spoke of her divorce. An old man, who I would bet had never uttered an unscripted word in church, stood at his pew and there in the darkness gave thanks to God for saving his life on Guadalcanal more than fifty years earlier. The stories differed greatly from one another, and who could judge how accurately the details were remembered? But each story testified to some *side* of God's faithfulness. From that miscellany of stories, a clearly defined figure began to emerge, not of any one of the tellers but of the Object of the tale. By the time the church service was to begin, we had already had church. We had already met God.

You may have anticipated my point. The sermon achieves a similar effect over time by means of repeated performances from a variety of perspectives. Tell it again, and again, and again, and you end up with God. Tell it again, and we discover our selves as well.

We have the high and dangerous calling of telling one last story in a world filled with lies. The story we tell must be true: true to the unfinished quality of human experience, true to the chaos, true to the church's rich life, but truest of all to the one who is, and who was, and who is to come, the Living One.

RECONCILIATION

Chapter Four

To What End?

Where is love more glorified than where she dwells
in the midst of her enemies?

Dietrich Bonhoeffer, *The Cost of Discipleship*

In Chapter Three I spoke of the art of preaching. The word "art" may have struck the reader as a somewhat optimistic if not idealistic descriptor of what goes on in churches every Sunday. Many do not think of the sermon as an artful rendering of Scripture or an imaginative evocation of the presence of Christ in our world. In the popular imagination the word "sermon" represents the antithesis of a gracious deployment of language in service of the gospel. According to Webster, the second meaning of "sermon" is "a serious talk on behavior, especially a long and tedious one."

If the sermon is an art-form that has just entered its twenty-first consecutive century of declining popularity, why do it? Why this dogged adherence to a pattern of communication whose formal characteristics appear to have outlived their usefulness? Why not several minutes of silence or small group discussion? Some rapidly growing churches are replacing the sermon with dramatic skits or film clips. Why persist in speaking the gospel in the midst of the assembly?

The Reconciling Imperative

The short answer is that Jesus sent his followers into the world to speak his message. The longer answer would include the examples of the prophets who spoke truth to power, the rabbis who explained the Scriptures in the synagogue, Jesus himself who announced the kingdom in the course of a sermon, and the apostle Paul who preached the cross as if there were no tomorrow.

For busy pastors the reasons for preaching are hazy at best. It is as if we have been preoccupied so long with capturing our culture's attention, that once we have it we have forgotten what we were supposed to say. Most reasons for preaching are oriented to knowledge and experience, to teaching and touching. Some preach to teach the Bible so that their hearers may accept its truths. Others preach to touch those whose lives have grown callused to grace, in the conviction that a good experience on Sunday can redeem the rest of the week.

But I am seeking the true end of words, which is the

ultimate purpose of the act of preaching. I am looking for
the animating principle, the life of the thing itself, but
also the larger thing in which all our little speeches fit. I
find it in the thesis sentence of the New Testament, 2 Corinthians 5:19:

> God was in Christ reconciling the world to himself, not
> counting their trespasses against them, and has en-
> trusted to us the message of reconciliation.

The mystery of God, captured in a message about what
God has done, is now entrusted to us. And what God has
done, on both a macro- and a microcosmic scale, is reconciliation.

At the heart of the universe lives a mysterious, hidden
Being whose very self is moved by love for all that he has
created. In the ministry, death, and resurrection of Jesus
of Nazareth, that Being has been revealed as one who is
perpetually turning toward us as if to welcome us home,
the way a mother and father open their arms to a way-
ward child. Whenever we preach, our sermons participate in this, God's definitive gesture toward the world.
The end of preaching is reconciliation.

If one were to answer the question "Why preach?" on
the basis of the first three chapters of this book, I suspect
we would reply as follows: We preach in order to communicate the distinctiveness of the Christian message in a
world of counter-messages and conflicting values. In an

era of wide-open pluralism, Christians must know who they are in the marketplace of religions and spiritualities. We must separate our story from the stories of the world and learn to live by our own script. In short, we preach to solidify our own identity.

But here is the paradox: We have this exclusive story of Israel, Jesus, and the church that belongs to the people of God. Yet written into the story as its most distinctive feature is its willingness to risk itself by embracing others. And all the preacher has to do is negotiate that paradox once a week in a public message!

Such a paradox can lead only to a thoughtful exploration, not a definitive resolution. But we are at least raising the hard question, one that homiletics rarely asks: How can our sermons participate in God's big plan? How can they become instruments of reconciliation?

We rightfully preach reconciliation locally, not because we are such good postmodernists, eschewing the Grand Narrative and all that, but because we are good pastors who know how to discern the signs of readiness among the congregation for difficult and challenging words. *Shalom* is not a monolith. It does not exist apart from people who are practicing it in a variety of forms and settings. Reconciliation looks different in its innumerable contexts — different in South Africa than in the United States, different in inter-Christian dialogue than in Christian-Muslim dialogue, different at a conference table than at a kitchen table.

To What End?

Yet Karl Barth reminds us that we preach "one mighty truth of the reconciliation," which in good homiletic fashion he divides into three phases.[1] First, the world *(kosmos)* is reconciled to God. To get a sense of *kosmos,* it helps to read 2 Corinthians 5:19 from a spacecraft looking back at a turquoise island in the night, or on the north rim of the Grand Canyon at sunrise, or from an airplane descending above Soweto, or from the midst of a chaotic ER. Early in the Gulf War, our choir sang Stainer's "God So Loved the World," and the juxtaposition of all that love and all that death was enough to bring tears to one's eyes. The roundness of the world can be proved photographically; the wholeness of the world can only be known by faith in one person's death.

Second, Barth says, persons are reconciled to persons and groups to groups. The social dimension of reconciliation is always news, even in the secular sphere. Several years ago our newspaper featured an enormous photograph on its front page. A black man and a white woman are sitting in her pastor's study at her church. The man's face is serene as he looks away from the camera and far beyond it, as if toward infinity. The woman's line of vision crosses his, but her eyes bore into the viewer, as if searching the faces of strangers for a little human understand-

1. Karl Barth, *Church Dogmatics,* trans. G. W. Bromiley, vol. 4, pt. 2, sec. 5 (Edinburgh: T. & T. Clark, 1958). On the three arenas of reconciliation, see pp. 314-15.

ing. Her expression is worried and her face puffy from crying. The man has just forgiven the woman for falsely accusing him of rape, an accusation that cost him eleven years of his life in a North Carolina prison. I would suspect that the account of the crime when it occurred was buried somewhere on the back pages of the newspaper, just one more anonymous outrage in a big city. But the act of forgiveness and the ensuing reconciliation and friendship between the two — that was page-one news. Why? Is it because the editors were looking for a feel-good story that day, or did they recognize a genuinely supernatural event when they saw one, one that had just reversed the natural course of human relationships?

Third, Barth says, human beings are reconciled within themselves. We were created to be unreservedly human and fully alive, which is God's glory. Because Jesus was the last Adam, Paul says in Romans and 1 Corinthians, he gathers in himself a new and reconstituted humanity. Thus to be fully human is not the consolation prize in God's parlor game; it is what God intended for us all along. To embrace one's humanity is not mere humanism but good theology.

We were not meant to be like Christian in Bunyan's *Pilgrim's Progress,* who makes his way through life doubled over by a backpack of unforgiven sins. We were not created to be torn by doubt, guilt, and personal conflict. The Greek word for forgive, *apheimi,* means to "send away," not the way we send away our laundry only to have

136

it returned a shade or two brighter than before, but the way we send away our trash into cyberspace, never to see it again. God's work of reconciliation is acknowledged when each person accepts God's forgiveness in Jesus Christ and embraces the fullness of his or her humanity.

Barth's account of the unity of divine and human reconciliation is well illustrated by the story of the reunion of Jacob and Esau, which is one of many such stories written into our script.[2] Jacob's whole life has been nothing but one big fight after another, beginning already in the womb when he and Esau fought it out for the status of firstborn. That is the narrative pattern Jacob's life will follow. He contends with his father, his father-in-law, his brother, his wives, and now (in Genesis 32) we find him preparing for another confrontation with his brother Esau, whom long ago he defrauded of his birthright.

The good news is that Esau is on his way for a family reunion. The bad news is that he is bringing four hundred men with him. Jacob is nervous. He compulsively assures anyone who will listen how much he wishes to look upon his brother's *face.* That night he is tormented by uneasy dreams. He has another fight, this time not with a relative but with the Lord, who wounds him with a blessing, after

2. For reflections on the story of Jacob and Esau, see John Paul Lederach, *The Journey Toward Reconciliation* (Scottdale, Pa.: Herald Press, 1999), pp. 17-26.

which Jacob can only say, "I have seen the face of God and lived."

The next day he finds himself standing before the brother he had cheated, twenty years of bad blood between them about to hemorrhage. Jacob has prudently divided his big family into two groups so that when Esau attacks one, the other might escape. With uncharacteristic courage, Jacob walks out in front of his retinue to meet his brother, bows seven times, and for a moment the narrative seems to stand still — until Esau shatters the tableau by charging toward him, presumably to slit his throat. But no, he kisses him and they fall into one another's arms in a rollicking embrace, like a pitcher and a catcher after a perfect game. This scene was so offensive to a later Jewish scribe that he changed the words "he kissed him" to "he bit him." But no! He kissed him. When Jacob offers his brother gifts to appease him, Esau sweetly replies, "I have enough, my brother; keep what you have for yourself." And Jacob, echoing his new relationship with God, replies, "Your face is like the face of God to me." One night he discovers the face of his God. The next morning he recognizes it in his brother.

Such stories, along with the Gospels and Paul, compose us as a people. Thanks to Paul, our faith is conditioned by the expectation of a reunion, that of Jews and Gentiles. The Lord came, says Paul in Ephesians, preaching peace to the Gentiles afar off and to the Jews close at hand. Christians now see the world through the lens of a broken wall and the eschatological reality of one new human race (Ephesians 2). We enact this hope every Sunday in rituals of confession and peace. Reconciliation is not a theological option, a specialized ministry, or the subject of an occasional sermon. Every congregation is a reconciling congregation.

In the Presence of My Enemy

If the world knows anything about Christians, it knows they stand for reconciliation. The church has already loaned its vocabulary of reconciliation to the nations, many of whom lack the conceptual resources for addressing past brutalities and the end of hostilities. Nations torn by violence and civil war have set up commissions on truth, peace, forgiveness, and reconciliation, borrowing generously from the Christian lexicon. Some, like South Africa and Rwanda, where victims have looked upon the face of their tormentors with unveiled horror, have carried out the process in explicitly theological terms. South Africa's quest for genuine reconciliation is unprecedented in modern history. On a somewhat reduced moral scale, heads of state and church leaders have apologized to injured groups for sins of historic proportions.

It is as if the whole world is waking to a hard lesson. Even when you win a war, wage a successful revolution, or vanquish your perpetrator, even when you apologize to your enemy, the enemy remains — on the same planet, often in the same zip code, always in your mind. The whole world is asking not "Who is my neighbor?" but "How do I live with my Enemy-Neighbor?"[3]

In some situations, "enemy" may be too strong a word. The faces of enemies have dissolved into a general structure of distrust of those who are simply *there*. In *The Cost of Discipleship*, Bonhoeffer evokes the banality of alienation when he writes, "We are separated from one another by an unbridgeable gulf of otherness and strangeness which resists all our attempts to overcome it by means of natural association or emotional or spiritual union. There is no way from one person to another."[4]

For years I have been taking my car to a garage owned and operated by Pakistanis. It is always a jolly experience marked by big smiles and small talk. Two years ago our newspaper ran a story on Muslims in our community who feel persecuted because of their religion, and to everyone's astonishment featured prominently in the article were our thoroughly Americanized, Tar Heel Pakistanis. We should have known. Behind their big smiles and our superficial small talk, they and we were the Other.

A post-colonial, post-Soviet environment, coupled

3. The phrase "Enemy-Neighbor" is Paul Ramsey's in *Basic Christian Ethics* (New York: Scribner's, 1950), p. 98.

4. Dietrich Bonhoeffer, *The Cost of Discipleship*, trans. R. H. Fuller (New York: Macmillan, 1959 [1937]), p. 98.

with American hegemony and the rise of Islamic radicalism, has oxygenated a blaze of ethnic and religious identity. The culture wars, which were once seen as academic skirmishes, have taken on a new and ominous meaning. Add to this, gender perspectives, issues of sexual orientation that have divided so many communions, and unresolved dilemmas of race, and you have an in-your-face awareness of the Other, not necessarily as *enemy* but as *Other.* We may make light of identity politics, but we must remember the millions of people who believe their identity is absolutely all they have in this world. If you don't protect your identity, who will?

In his book *Exclusion and Embrace,* Miroslav Volf asks the critical question, which might be paraphrased as follows: What is the defining mark of human life — is it the undeniable fact of that special identity that makes *me* me and *you* you, and our group what it is and their group something other, or is it the equally undeniable fact of some wider bond of humanity that we hold in common?[5] Must identity always trump community?

That which produces both pride and conflict among us is *difference.* In the beginning, God created a world teaming with difference, and behold, it was very good. So, why is it killing us now? Why does difference underlie ev-

5. Miroslav Volf, *Exclusion and Embrace* (Nashville: Abingdon, 1996), pp. 35-68. "It may not be too much to claim that the future of the world will depend on how we deal with identity and difference" (p. 20).

ery imaginable social conflict? The answer is theological. It is because we are establishing our identity not in relation to the Father in whose image we were created or the Son in whose likeness we have been recreated, but by differentiating ourselves from our fellow creatures. I know I am white because you are brown. I know I am straight because you are gay. I know I am Western because you prostrate yourself toward the East. For a long time we held back the flood of *difference* with the political myth of the melting pot and the theological cliché of inclusiveness. We pretended that once the doors of the church close all differences evaporate.

But now the dam is bursting with difference. That which was given as an abundant gift is now dogged by conflict, violence, and hate. Long ago, Augustine characterized the state of human nature as "a chronic condition of civil war." More than a millennium later, the social philosopher Thomas Hobbes described civil society as *bellum omnium contra omnes,* "the war of all against all." The linguistics scholar Deborah Tannen dubs contemporary America "the Argument Culture," the key to which she says is not multiplicity but polarization. Then speaking of the media and its voracious appetite for violence in all its forms, she adds, "No fight, no news."[6]

6. Deborah Tannen, *The Argument Culture* (New York: Random House, 1998), pp. 22, 28, 30. Volf adds to her analysis his own mordant observation of "an insatiable appetite for brutality among ordinary people" (p. 86).

A generation ago, civil rights activists discovered the same sad truth about America's attention span. The civil rights movement showcased the power of community, the fire of the black church, and some of the most eloquent oratory in American history, but its leaders soon discovered that if the movement was not accompanied by telegenic acts of violence for the evening news, the country quickly lost interest. As then, so today, no fight, no news.

Today, the instinct for polarization is trained outward toward "the enemies of freedom." The language of terror divides the world and the regimes of the world into good and evil, as once the world was divided into free and communist sectors. Such rhetoric dominates the script of politics and the media and, to an extent and with a force that cannot be measured, threatens to silence the voices of peace.

And how is it in the church?

The Reconciling Sermon

When I arrived in my second parish, the chief deacon of the congregation insisted on reviewing the entire membership roster with me. In retrospect, it was touchingly naive how he went down the list saying after each name, "No problem," "no problem" — the implication being that a good church does not have problems. A month later as I reviewed the same list, I was shell-shocked by the problems — by the bad blood, battles, and betrayals in my little congregation.

The reconciling sermon begins with pastoral discernment of the way things are. And the way things are is that many of us are living in the presence of our enemies. We preach reconciliation amidst a jumble of unfinished business, among people who are beginning new lives willy-nilly without having completed the old.

We preachers ourselves bear the burdens of estrangement. Who in our own family has escaped divorce, abuse, or conflict? According to an Alban Institute researcher, up to one half of clergy come from what he terms "dysfunctional or traumatically unloving families."[7]

We preach God's love to those who are staggering through loveless relationships. We preach forgiveness to injured parties who possess a moral right to say "Never again." Worst of all, we preach reconciliation to those who, either consciously or unconsciously, seize upon our words as permission for continued sin. Of them the Scripture says, "They crucify the Son of God afresh." Nowhere do you see the vulnerability of the church more clearly than when it gathers up its authority and announces the forgiveness of sins.

This is the way things are.

7. Roy M. Oswald, *Finding Leaders for Tomorrow's Churches* (n.p.: Alban Institute, 1993), p. 60.

The second move in a reconciling sermon occurs when this same pastor, chastened by the way things are and yet moved by the hope of peace — tells the truth. This may be a surprising statement since many think of reconciliation as a means of avoiding the truth or as a process that is derailed by hard truths.

A young Reinhold Niebuhr confessed to his diary how hard it is to tell unpleasant truths to people you have come to love. I confess that it was always easier for me to tell the truth about racism in South Africa than in my own town, easier to love an abstract enemy than an opponent in the church.

Miroslav Volf rightly insists that theologically, the will to embrace takes precedence over "truth" in the abstract or the mapping of good and evil.[8] But reconciliation cannot occur apart from truth-telling. When Desmond Tutu submitted the final report of the Truth and Reconciliation Commission, he said, "Fellow South Africans, accept this report as a way, an indispensable way of healing, where *we have looked the beast in the eye.*"[9] This is what Kierkegaard had in mind when he insisted, "The wound

---

8. Volf, *Exclusion and Embrace,* p. 29. On the priority of forgiveness see also L. Gregory Jones, *Embodying Forgiveness* (Grand Rapids: Eerdmans, 1995), pp. 5, 110.

9. Reported in the *Washington Post,* October 30, 1998, my italics. Rosa Luxembourg said, "The most revolutionary deed is and always will remain to say out loud what is the case" (quoted in Volf, *Exclusion and Embrace,* p. 235).

must be kept open in order that the eternal may heal it," and Jonathan Edwards, when he compared preaching to lancing a boil.

The liturgical analogue to phase two in the reconciling sermon is the confession of sins. The preacher begins by confessing to God his or her own hidden allegiance to the ways of violence. The preacher is personally acquainted with violent impulses, rage, frustration, and episodes of lashing out at others. The minister acknowledges he is willing to use power in order to advance his career or get his own way. Sometimes, by the preacher's silence, she lends support to the nation's illegitimate exercise of violence. Our hands are not clean, our hearts are not pure.

The preacher must also confess that Christianity is deeply implicated in the violence of the world, especially the violence perpetrated in the name of Jesus or Christian values. When a Jewish colleague confronts me with Luther's tract against the Jews, the road to reconciliation for us runs *through* those terrible words, not around them. Christians continue to legitimate domestic violence and the oppression of gays in the name of Christian values. Some Christians have hitched their mission to politics at home and military power abroad. They have sponsored what continues to be the most segregated hour in American life. The moral failings of their priests are breathtaking.

But the truth about the church cannot be reduced to

a box score of its scandals and successes. For the church simply exists, in John Calvin's words, as a lacerated body in the world. And that, too, constitutes its truth. Its struggles for reconciliation in conflicted areas such as Chile, the Philippines, East Germany, and Hungary, if not counted as unambiguous successes, still witness to the church's strength and its willingness to suffer in a dangerous world.[10]

The preacher tells the truth — about hate, violence, suffering, pride, idolatry, all of it — but the sermon's truth is not the same as political or social analysis. Our truth-telling always occurs in relation to God's revelation of truth and our baptismal identity, because who we are in Jesus Christ is as much the truth about us as is our complicity in the sin of the world.

The third phase in a reconciling sermon occurs when the speaker preaches the good news in Jesus Christ and offers with it signs and gestures of reconciliation. Despite Protestantism's muscular confidence in the word, the preacher should not think that any one sermon is bound to achieve "world peace" or reconciliation among entrenched antagonists. Sometimes the lacerations are so deep and irrevocable that only a separate peace is possible. Esau and Jacob embraced and then went their separate ways. In Acts 15 the reconciliation of the two church

10. Robert Schreiter, *Reconciliation* (Maryknoll, N.Y.: Orbis, 1992), p. 66.

factions entailed a division of labor. Contemporary Christians sometimes "separate" or divorce and establish lives of wholeness apart from one another.

It is sometimes the case that the Other is so inaccessible that literal life together will never be possible. We can have healing of memories and we may forgive the dead, but reconciliation with them is impossible, because the dead cannot forgive us back. We can do no more than preach *toward* reconciliation. By consistently gesturing in the direction of reconciliation while at the same time acknowledging its partial and imperfect character, the preacher reveals something of the ultimate purpose of the gospel.

The gospel of reconciliation is the gospel of freely given grace. But grace is not grace if its recipients must deserve it or if by their attitude or behavior they somehow set it in motion. Every attempt to impose an order of prerequisites on grace by insisting on contrition, confession, shame, and repentance or by limiting forgivable offenses to a specified number — say, seven — fails before Jesus' own example. He healed some people before they asked for help. He forgave others before they repented. Sometimes, his kindness evoked repentance and faith, sometimes it did not. He himself died forgiving his unrepentant torturers. His death at the hands of his enemies is the event by which God continues to make peace with the whole world. If reconciliation is not free, it is not of God.

Nevertheless, preaching toward reconciliation is one of the most dangerous of all pastoral activities, dangerous not to the preacher but to those who take his or her words seriously.

If every Christian is compelled to forgive seventy times seven, what message does such generosity send to men who repeatedly abuse women or women who are repeatedly counseled to forgive them? Does it condone the sin? Does it imply that the suffering of the victim is not important? In the parable in which Jesus enjoins unlimited forgiveness (Matt. 18:23-35), the king does *not* forgive the unforgiving servant but exercises his royal judgment and turns him over to the torturers. The servant who was forgiven abused the gift by failing to forgive his fellow servant.[11]

Forgiveness is, or should be, a stepping-stone toward reconciliation by which two people or groups are enabled to live together in peace.[12] Reconciliation is the final destination of alienated people or groups who have freely offered and received forgiveness. Therefore it cannot be imposed by the stronger of the two sides. When one party forgives the other as a consequence of emo-

11. See the comments of Susan E. Hylen made in the context of domestic violence in "Forgiveness and Life in Community," *Interpretation* 54, no. 2 (April 2000): 146-57.

12. Jones, *Embodying Forgiveness,* p. 5. In "Crafting Communities of Forgiveness," *Interpretation* 54, no. 2 (April 2000), he calls reconciliation the telos of Christian forgiveness (p. 122).

tional manipulation or a power imbalance, the act of for-giveness cannot lead to the mutual embrace of reconcili-ation, for one of the parties has been "faking it" from the beginning of the process. Those who forgive in such cir-cumstances may attain a measure of inner peace by let-ting go of their hatred for the Other. Many have reported that once they forgave their oppressor they felt "free" for the first time in a long time, but because the Other was either inaccessible or unrepentant they did not, and could not, experience reconciliation in its fullest sense, but only hope for it.

All this is to say that the preacher must not be too glib with the words "forgiveness" and "reconciliation" lest the sermon give the impression that grace comes cheap or that it is easy. When Bonhoeffer coined his famous phrase he was not qualifying God's grace as much as re-minding us that forgiveness always costs someone some-thing. It cost God his son. It costs those who practice it the risk of further injury. We dare to use such language only because these words have been paid for.

How to resolve the dilemma of free versus cheap grace? When God moved freely toward the world in grace, I believe the church was included in the gift both as the instrument of peace and as the laboratory in which God's people try it out. You might say God's free grace comes with a kit for experimenting with it. The kit includes worship, the sacraments, and pastoral care. The community is larger than the sum of our individual failures to practice grace. Even when the preacher gets the gospel wrong, the liturgy gets it right. Even when the words of forgiveness stick in our throats, the liturgy speaks them through us. When I am angry with my neighbor, sure enough, when I spin around in my pew to share the Peace of the Lord, who is it but that very neighbor to whom I must extend a hand or, God forbid, an embrace. Even when I don't feel *forgiven*, the liturgy says, "In Christ you are forgiven." When I don't feel like *forgiving*, there are others around me saying it on my behalf until it is possible for me to join them. In the combustion of word and touch, miniature "new creations" are exploding around the sanctuary. Perhaps they are insignificant when compared to the problems of ethnic cleansing or apartheid, but these ritualized practices establish a pattern for distinctively Christian behavior in the world.

Contrary to much Protestant theology, the gospel does not consist in a few riveting pronouncements from the pulpit. The word of God usually does *not* knife through history and impale its hearers on their own inauthentic existence. The ministry of the word is an endless card game played out among people who never stop talking with and caring for one another. In some communities the process is called mutual care, in others it is called gossip. Preachers have a lot to learn about reconciliation from the people who practice it on the ground. "There are believers," says John Howard Yoder, "who for Jesus' sake do ordinary social things differently.

They fraternize trans-ethnically; they share their bread; they forgive one another." Their churches are outposts of *shalom*.[13]

Without the community, one cannot absorb the truth or use it to any good effect. The naked truth about sin is a horror. The word of forgiveness is a non-starter for those bereft of community. Imagine, if you can, sitting in one of the town halls in South Africa as a policeman coolly describes how he and his fellows hung your brother above a fire, interrogated him, and scorched him till he died. The judge does not pronounce absolution, only amnesty, and the killer walks free. Of this process Peter Storey writes, "It is an area more consistent with Calvary than the courtroom."[14] By the same token, if you yourself are the murderer, rapist, abuser, or despiser of humanity, of what saving health is it for you to be impaled on the word "forgiven" in isolation from the eucharistic table and the joy of the forgiven community?

Most sermons contain an analysis of evil based on the

13. John Howard Yoder, *Body Politics* (Nashville: Discipleship Resources, 1992), p. 75. On the church as an outpost of *shalom* see Richard John Neuhaus, *Freedom for Ministry* (New York: Harper and Row, 1979), p. 63.

14. Peter Storey, "A Different Kind of Justice: Truth and Reconciliation in South Africa," *The Christian Century* 114, no. 25 (September 10-17, 1997): 793. The *Report* of the Truth and Reconciliation Commission, with a foreword by Desmond Tutu, is indispensable reading (vol. 1, Capetown: Juta, 1998).

Bible's condemnation of sin and the preacher's awareness of the human condition. Most Christian sermons announce God's intervention in Jesus Christ, employing a variety of metaphors: He has forgiven us, healed us, defeated sin and death, promised eternal life. Most sermons encourage the listener to accept the good news, usually at the level of a personal relationship with God. This stage is the last camp before the climber reaches the summit. Most sermons, however, do not make the final ascent. The preacher turns around at this point, satisfied with the view, and heads down the mountain. Too many gospel sermons do not make the ultimate gospel gesture by celebrating God's reconciliation of enemies in the church and the world. Which means that such sermons have no basis on which to encourage their hearers to seek the appropriate level of reconciliation in their lives. They come very near the true end of words, but fall short of its glory.

The Language of Peace

Preachers have been given a language with which to express God's reconciliation, but they find it difficult to say in the Argument Culture; for "the war of all against all" rages within the culture of the church as well as the world around it. Where earlier generations fought it out over the virgin birth and the divinity of Christ, today's Christians clash over social and political issues such as abortion, homosexuality, and war, but with similar results. The rhetoric of conflict perches like a vulture on the language of peace. Caliban's lament in *The Tempest* echoes the Christian irony: "You taught me language, and my profit on't/Is, I know how to curse. . . ."

The Western rhetorical tradition to which the sermon is heir is agonistic, that is, conflictual, oppositional. It was born in contest. One scholar describes classical training in rhetoric as the "brutal disciplining of [male] pupils" and "the programmatically combative oral testing of knowledge."[15] In 1 Corinthians 1 Paul renounces the dominant rhetorical paradigm of his day, which would have included, above all, the *contest*. Skilled as he was in rhetorical technique, Paul bids farewell to "the debater[s] of this age."

Yet the conflict model of rhetoric persisted throughout much of the church's history. Many of the great preachers from Tertullian, Cyprian, and Augustine to Charles Grandison Finney were originally lawyers and professional orators whose business it was to win arguments. Before he became a bishop, Augustine held the Imperial Chair of Rhetoric in Milan. Although he renounced rhetoric in the *Confessions*, many years later he "armed" Christian preachers with principles learned from Cicero. After his conversion, Charles Finney moved

15. Walter J. Ong, *Fighting for Life* (Ithaca, N.Y.: Cornell University Press, 1981), p. 25.

his practice from the courtroom to the auditorium, where, using the very same tools of persuasion, he continued to win impressive verdicts.

Our predecessors were trained to *defend* the truth and to *demolish* the claims of the opposition, to *attack* every weakness, to *shoot down* all their arguments, to *score* points, and to *win.*

The combative tradition continues among postmodernists but in different terms and with radically different assumptions. The postmodernists have an expression: "To speak is to fight." If the essence of language is to establish identities by marking differences, the expression makes sense. According to Frederic Jameson, language is less a process of transmitting information than "taking of tricks" and trumping the adversary.[16]

One encounters the agonistic rhetoric in more pious but no less sophisticated tones in the hallways of a divinity school or in the pages of prominent theological journals. The editorials of one, in particular, skewer opponents with contempt and sarcasm, scoring theological bull's-eyes in debates over such matters as Christian unity or the apostolic succession. And what could be

16. "To speak . . . ," comes from Jean-François Lyotard, *The Postmodern Condition: A Report on Knowledge,* trans. Geoff Bennington and Brian Massumi (Minneapolis: University of Minnesota Press, 1984 [1979]), p. 10. Jameson is quoted in Lyotard, p. xi. On combative rhetoric, see George Lakoff and Mark Johnson, *Metaphors We Live By* (Chicago: University of Chicago Press, 1980), p. 4.

more agonistic (agony provoking) than the church's conversations on sexuality?

You might say fighting with words at least is preferable to fighting with tanks, and who would disagree? Indeed, the most important rhetorician of the twentieth century, the philosopher Kenneth Burke, defined rhetoric as a means of inducing cooperation among creatures who communicate by means of symbols (words). Preachers must never forget that their vocation participates in an overarching alternative to physical violence, which only highlights the contradiction inherent in a great deal of religious discourse. How can the message of peace employ the rhetorical techniques of war? How do you talk like a Christian?

Unfortunately, our most famous progenitors offer little help. Church Fathers such as Tertullian and Jerome were masters of invective. Martin Luther was a skilled polemicist who was not above characterizing his opponents as a variety of barnyard animals. But one should not think Luther's model of preaching was the catapult that lobs missiles over the barricade, for on more than one occasion he compared the preacher to a woman who breast-feeds her young.

Perhaps the best example of the move from violent speech to the language of love is found in the Psalms. The Psalms are as loaded with imprecation as any religious documents, but in Psalm 59 we are provided with a vivid contrast between two forms of speech and the abrupt movement from one to the other. In this psalm the evil-doers howl like dogs, bellow with their mouths, snarl with their lips, lie, and curse. But to the growls of his opponents the psalmist juxtaposes his chosen discourse, which is a song to God.

> They roam about for food,
>> and growl if they do not get their fill.
> But I will sing of thy might;
>> I will sing aloud of thy steadfast love
>>> in the morning.   (vv. 15-16)

No fewer than four times the writer characterizes his language as singing. He does not achieve reconciliation with his enemy, but, taking our cue from the psalmist, might not the quest for peace begin with a song of praise to the One who transcends all difference?

Perhaps it is too facile simply to call for speech that is inclusive, collegial, and non-authoritarian, for these categories have themselves become slogans along the barricades. The charitable preacher "will begin the slow, often tedious process of learning the presumptions, conventions, and idioms needed to make others' views intelligible." The reconciling sermon "entails both a willingness to listen to differences and a willingness to hear those differences in their fullness."[17] In the end, the preacher

17. Stephen E. Fowl, *Engaging Scripture* (Oxford: Blackwell, 1998),

strives to make the language of the sermon true to its subject by deploying words in a such a way that they are consistent with the ministry of reconciliation.[18]

No single homiletical form can ensure the desired effect of reconciliation. Colleagues in the field of homiletics have asserted that narrative is less conducive to conflict than other sermon forms. They may have a point, though it depends on what kind of stories one tells and to what end. Not individual stories, but the ongoing narration of Christian identity lays the foundation for dialogue. Other homileticians favor the inductive method as a means of avoiding authoritarianism. Linear thinking and the enumeration of points and PowerPoints are said to be inherently hierarchical and therefore oppressive to the listener. Still others have advocated conversational preaching as a means of allowing those whose voices have been silenced to be heard. All these (unprovable) claims contain elements of truth. But I am hesitant to make a law of these theories because I suspect the reconciling sermon's roots go deeper than form. The reconciling sermon originates in the reconciling preacher and the constancy of his or her theological vision.

Some preachers feel so besieged by forces beyond their

p. 89. Fowl is speaking of the "charitable interpreter" in the context of biblical interpretation.

18. "Make the language true to its subject" is Wendell Berry's advice to poets in *Standing By Words* (San Francisco: North Point, 1983), p. 29.

control that even though they have been entrusted with the message of the open palm they deliver it with a closed fist. There are preachers whose agenda, whether overt or hidden, is driven by a compulsive need to prove the superiority of "us" and the inferiority of "them," and no amount of fiddling with the sermon's form will change that.

But there are also Christians who maintain a constancy of vision that includes the reconciliation of enemies. A little over a decade ago, Nobel laureate Mairead Corrigan Maguire wrote an open letter to her enemy, fellow Catholic Gerry Adams, the president of Sinn Fein. Adams has long defended the IRA's "armed struggle" on the basis of Christian just-war theory. The letter is titled "There Is No Just War," and what I find extraordinary about this document (very much a sermon) is the way in which Maguire combines the two essential gestures of reconciling speech. She tells the truth, and she does so with open arms. She exposes the misery of the armed struggle as well as the poverty of the church's defense of it. She grieves over the church's failure to prepare future priests and preachers to speak nonviolently. "The Christian message is simple," she writes: "Tell people to stop killing each other and to start loving one another, including their enemies. It is simply not being said."

But second, even as she tells the truth, Maguire's letter verbally embraces her enemy. She does not condescend to him morally but addresses him as a brother on the basis of their shared Christian faith. She does not make arguments but re-narrates a Catholic Christian identity, going so far as to reflect on the conditions under which Adams should receive the Eucharist. She concludes, "In a community as deeply divided as ours, shouldn't every Christian take the initiative and move forward toward reconciliation? Christ has called us to take that step. *Shalom, Mairead.*"[19]

A reconciling sermon may not always be *about* forgiveness and reconciliation, but it will make two reconciling provisions: it will patiently seek to understand the position of the Other, even when that Other *is* the audience or sits among the audience, and it will leave the door ajar to a future that no one, including the preacher, can fully comprehend.

These and other provisions of the reconciling sermon are clearly evident in the collected sermons of Martin Luther King Jr. Taken as a whole, they reveal a reconciling profile in one of the twentieth century's greatest preachers. In these sermons the preacher King tells the truth about the sins of racism, idolatry, militarism, and violence. As Desmond Tutu would put it, he is not afraid to look the beast in the eye. Yet he does so in a way that is remarkably generous toward his enemies. Where it is possible to "explain" racism as a symptom of fear or some

19. Mairead Corrigan Maguire, "There Is No Just War: A Letter to Gerry Adams," in *The Vision of Peace,* ed. John Dear (Maryknoll, N.Y.: Orbis, 1999), pp. 28-31.

other psychological or cultural disorder, he does so. He often takes time to understand and articulate the white Southerner's anxiety in the face of change. He makes his judgments on racism and war against the backdrop of God's profound love for the world, a theological awareness which lends to his sermons a brooding sense of pathos. In re-reading them, one is reminded that the emotion most characteristic of the prophet is not anger but sorrow. He tells the truth but rarely in bitterness of spirit and never with contempt for the Other. His truth-telling is pervaded by a sense of tragedy.

In his sermons King also announces God's intervention by evoking themes related to the Exodus and/or Christ's redemption of the world. In his grammar, redemption always has a future tense. The tone of promise with which he inflects his message is the result not of his native optimism but of serious theological reflection on the scope of redemption. Although embroiled in many local conflicts, King never took his eye off the *kosmos* and the universal fact of reconciliation. The victory he promises will be big enough to include victims *and* victimizers, the segregated *and* the segregators, in the beloved community. King fought as hard as anyone in America for new laws, but his sermons palpably yearn for the new thing that rises just beyond the law's guarantees. And for Martin Luther King that new thing was the peculiarly American expression of God's reconciliation of the world through Jesus Christ.

In South Africa, the reconciling sermon has been taken up by Desmond Tutu, who in the midst of social and political turmoil continues to preach his favorite text, Ephesians 2:14: "For he is our peace; in his flesh he has made both groups into one and has broken down the dividing wall, that is, the hostility between us."

Neither Tutu nor King presents a systematic theology of reconciliation, but their sermons offer a model of alternative Christian discourse. King draws his hope from the "big picture" of God's cosmic reconciliation. He grounds his message in creation, the image of God, redemption, and the anticipation of a new community. Tutu, on the other hand, looks to the community of believers to model reconciling activities that will one day lead to the renewal of politics.[20] Focusing on communal faithfulness, his ministry of the word bypasses liberation and Marxist models based on conflict. In the post-apartheid era, he has championed reconciliation above retribution. If the people of God will only claim their identity, they (we) will *be* the alternative to racism and violence and thereby constitute a powerful witness in the world. The sermons of King and Tutu embolden us all. To ordinary preachers like us they say, By God's grace, it can be done!

The reconciling sermon is broadly narrative rather

20. Michael Battle, *Reconciliation: The Ubuntu Theology of Desmond Tutu* (Cleveland: Pilgrim, 1997), on Ephesians 2:14, p. 97. On the communal model, p. 157.

than persuasive or argumentative. Instead of starting from the errors of our enemies, the sermon narrates the Lord's truth as we know and practice it. Our sermons need not demolish "the world," because the world is the same creation over which God grieves and the very same world for which Christ gave his life. Our leading homiletical subject is not "they," by which we character-ize a shadowy, collective Other, but *we:* "We believe, teach, and confess."

And finally, the key to forming people for discipleship lies not with the hortatory but with the indicative mood of address. Ultimately, it is the promise of the gospel and the power of the Holy Spirit and not the nagging of the preacher that makes for change in people's lives. For preachers, as with parents, the time eventually comes when the powerful "You must" gives way to an even more powerful "You are."

Reconciling speech is not our native language. It comes from outside us in the testimony of Scripture and the lyricism of worship, languages that even the believer may find awkward to use in the marketplace. But because of our baptism and the work of the Holy Spirit, this new way of talking now wells up within us and our communi-ties. We preach *toward* reconciliation but also *from* a res-ervoir of forgiveness that, had we not received it and shared it among ourselves, we could not speak it. We now participate in something larger and better than our in-herently violent disposition toward enemies. This something Paul terms the ministry of reconciliation. We have found our role in God's script at last.

With such knowledge comes freedom. In all public speech, the speaker experiences a latent and at the very least structural antagonism vis-à-vis the audience, which is "out there" as critic, consumer, and the performer's ultimate Other. In Christ, however, we are released from treating our fellow believers as an audience to be placated, persuaded, or impressed. For they are the same people with whom the preacher shares the handshake or embrace of peace. The reconciling sermon is the rhetorical equivalent of this liturgical act. We will love our listeners with our words as God has loved us in the word made flesh, and in so doing we will discover a surprising new power of expression, one that does not "win over" but "joins with" its audience. I can think of no greater source of freedom in the pulpit than the preacher's own reconciliation with the ultimate source of speech.

In the seventeenth-century classic *The Country Parson,* George Herbert warns his readers that "sermons are dangerous things; that none goes out of church as he came in." Sermons are dangerous things: After hearing a reconciling sermon, two people with a troubled marriage decide to give it another chance. A teenager shocks her parents by bringing her Muslim friend home for dinner. The local bigot softens his stance toward co-workers in the shop. None of these people came to church expecting anything to change in themselves or their world. But something did, and now nothing can ever be the same again. What if every sermon exposed its listeners to this danger, that of being fundamentally changed by the message of reconciliation?

Violence puts an end to words except as instruments of domination and difference. We seek the true end of words, which is that one mighty truth for which Jesus prayed in the upper room and Paul proclaimed to Jew and Gentile, slave and free, man and woman. It already indwells those who seek it.

In the Argument Culture of the twenty-first century, who will speak a word of peace, if not the preacher?

Select Bibliography

Anderson, Bernard W. *From Creation to New Creation: Old Testament Perspectives.* Minneapolis: Fortress, 1994.

Aristotle. *Poetics.* Translated by Ingram Bywater. New York: Modern Library, 1954.

Auerbach, Erich. *Mimesis: The Representation of Reality in Western Literature.* Translated by Willard Trask. New York: Doubleday, 1953.

Augustine. *On Christian Doctrine.* Translated by D. W. Robertson Jr. Indianapolis: Bobbs-Merrill, 1958.

Badcock, Gary D. *The Way of Life: A Theology of Christian Vocation.* Grand Rapids: Eerdmans, 1998.

Baldwin, James. *The Fire Next Time.* New York: Dial, 1963.

Barth, Karl. *Church Dogmatics.* Vol. 4. Translated by G. W. Bromiley. Edinburgh: T. & T. Clark, 1958.

————. *Deliverance to the Captives.* Translated by Marguerite Wiser. Westport, Conn.: Greenwood, 1979.

Battle, Michael. *Reconciliation: The Ubuntu Theology of Desmond Tutu.* Cleveland: Pilgrim, 1997.

Bellah, Robert N. "Christian Faithfulness in a Pluralist World." In *Postmodern Theology: Christian Faith in a Pluralist World,* edited by Frederic B. Burnham. New York: Harper and Row, 1989.

Bellah, Robert N., et al. *Habits of the Heart: Individualism and Commitment in American Life.* New York: Harper and Row, 1985.

Berry, Wendell. *Standing by Words.* San Francisco: North Point Press, 1983.

Billing, Einar. *Our Calling.* Translated by Conrad Bergendorf. 1907. Reprint, Philadelphia: Fortress, 1964.

Bonhoeffer, Dietrich. *The Cost of Discipleship.* Translated by R. H. Fuller. 1937. Reprint, New York: Macmillan, 1959.

————. *Letters and Papers from Prison.* Translated by Reginald Fuller, Frank Clarke, et al. Edited by Eberhard Bethge. 1953. Reprint, New York: Macmillan, 1971.

————. *Worldly Preaching.* Translated with an introduction by Clyde E. Fant. New York: Thomas Nelson, 1975.

Brilioth, Yngve. *A Brief History of Preaching.* Translated by Karl E. Mattson. 1945. Reprint, Philadelphia: Fortress, 1965.

Budde, Michael. *The (Magic) Kingdom of God: Christianity and Global Culture Industries.* Boulder: Westview, 1997.

Bunyan, John. *Grace Abounding.* New York: Oxford University Press, 1988.

Burnham, Frederic B., ed. *Postmodern Theology: Christian Faith in a Pluralist World.* San Francisco: Harper and Row, 1989.

Chesterton, Gilbert K. *Orthodoxy.* 1908. Reprint, New York: Doubleday, 1990.

Coombs, Marie Theresa, and Francis Kelly Nemeck. *Called by God: A Theology of Vocation and Lifelong Commitment.* Collegeville, Minn.: Liturgical Press, 1992.

Craddock, Fred B. *Overhearing the Gospel: Preaching and*

Teaching the Faith to Persons Who Have Already Heard. Nashville: Abingdon, 1978.

———. *Preaching.* Nashville: Abingdon, 1985.

Cunningham, David S. *Faithful Persuasion: In Aid of a Rhetoric of Christian Theology.* Notre Dame, Ind.: University of Notre Dame Press, 1991.

Dyrness, William A. *How Does America Hear the Gospel?* Grand Rapids: Eerdmans, 1989.

Forsyth, P. T. *Positive Preaching and the Modern Mind.* Grand Rapids: Baker, 1980. Originally published in 1907 as *Positive Preaching and Modern Mind.*

Fowl, Stephen E. *Engaging Scripture: A Model for Theological Interpretation.* Oxford: Blackwell, 1998.

———, ed. *The Theological Interpretation of Scripture.* Oxford: Blackwell, 1997.

Fowl, Stephen E., and L. Gregory Jones. *Reading in Communion: Scripture and Ethics in Christian Life.* Grand Rapids: Eerdmans, 1991.

Frank, Arthur W. *The Wounded Storyteller: Body, Illness, and Ethics.* Chicago: University of Chicago Press, 1995.

Fukuyama, Francis. *The End of History and the Last Man.* New York: Free Press, 1992.

Gergen, Kenneth J. *The Saturated Self: Dilemmas of Identity in Contemporary Life.* New York: Basic, 1991.

Gleick, James. *Faster: The Acceleration of Just About Everything.* New York: Pantheon, 1999.

Griffiths, Paul J. *Religious Reading: The Place of Reading in the Practice of Religion.* New York: Oxford University Press, 1999.

Hauerwas, Stanley. *Dispatches from the Front: Theological Engagement with the Secular.* Durham, N.C.: Duke University Press, 1994.

Hays, Richard B. "Salvation by Trust? Reading the Bible Faithfully." *The Christian Century* 114, no. 7 (February 26, 1997): 218-23.

Holifield, E. Brooks. *A History of Pastoral Care in America: From Salvation to Self-Realization, 1570-1970.* Nashville: Abingdon, 1983.

Hylen, Susan E. "Forgiveness and Life in Community." *Interpretation* 54, no. 2 (April 2000): 146-57.

Jeffrey, Paul. "Telling the Truth." *The Christian Century* 112, no. 25 (Aug. 30–Sept 6, 1995): 804-6.

Johnson, Clifton H., ed. *God Struck Me Dead.* Philadelphia: Pilgrim, 1969.

Johnson, Luke Timothy. "Imagining the World Scripture Imagines." In *Theology and Scriptural Imagination,* edited by L. Gregory Jones and James J. Buckley. Oxford: Blackwell, 1998.

Jones, L. Gregory. "Crafting Communities of Forgiveness." *Interpretation* 54, no. 2 (April 2000): 121-34.

———. *Embodying Forgiveness: A Theological Analysis.* Grand Rapids: Eerdmans, 1995.

Jones, L. Gregory, and James J. Buckley, eds. *Theology and Scriptural Imagination.* Oxford: Blackwell, 1998.

King, Martin Luther, Jr. *Strength to Love.* Philadelphia: Fortress, 1963.

Kugel, James L., and Rowan A. Greer. *Early Biblical Interpretation.* Philadelphia: Westminister, 1986.

Lakoff, George, and Mark Johnson. *Metaphors We Live By.* Chicago: University of Chicago Press, 1980.

Lanham, Richard A. *Style: An Anti-Textbook.* New Haven: Yale University Press, 1974.

Select Bibliography

Lash, Nicholas. *Theology on the Road to Emmaus.* London: SCM Press, 1986.

Lederach, John Paul. *The Journey Toward Reconciliation.* Scottdale, Pa.: Herald, 1999.

Lewis, C. S. *Surprised by Joy: The Shape of My Early Life.* New York: Harcourt Brace, 1955.

Lindbeck, George A. *The Nature of Doctrine: Religion and Theology in a Postliberal Age.* Philadelphia: Westminster, 1984.

Lischer, Richard, ed. *The Company of Preachers: Wisdom on Preaching, Augustine to the Present.* Grand Rapids: Eerdmans, 2002.

———. "The Limits of Story." *Interpretation* 38, no. 1 (January 1984): 26-38.

———. *The Preacher King: Martin Luther King, Jr. and the Word that Moved America.* New York: Oxford University Press, 1995.

Lochman, Jan Milic. *Reconciliation and Liberation: Challenging a One-Dimensional View of Salvation.* Translated by David Lewis. Philadelphia: Fortress, 1980.

Long, Thomas G. *The Witness of Preaching.* Louisville: Westminster/John Knox, 1989.

Loughlin, Gerard. *Telling God's Story: Bible, Church and Narrative Theology.* Cambridge: Cambridge University Press, 1996.

Luther, Martin. *Luther's Works.* Vol. 35. Edited by E. Theodore Bachmann. Philadelphia: Fortress, 1960. And Vol. 51. Edited by John Dobberstein, 1959.

Lyotard, Jean-François. *The Postmodern Condition: A Report on Knowledge.* Translated by Geoff Bennington and Brian Massumi. 1979. Reprint, Minneapolis: University of Minnesota Press, 1984.

MacIntyre, Alasdair. *After Virtue: A Study in Moral Theory.* 2nd ed. Notre Dame, Ind.: University of Notre Dame Press, 1984.

Maclean, Norman. *A River Runs through It.* 1976. Reprint, New York: Pocket, 1992.

Maguire, Mairead Corrigan. *The Vision of Peace: Faith and Hope in Northern Ireland.* Maryknoll, N.Y.: Orbis, 1999.

Neuhaus, Richard John. *Freedom for Ministry.* New York: Harper and Row, 1979.

Niebuhr, H. Richard, with Daniel Day Williams and James M. Gustafson. *The Purpose of the Church and Its Ministry: Reflections on the Aims of Theological Education.* New York: Harper and Brothers, 1956.

Niebuhr, Reinhold. *Leaves from the Notebook of a Tamed Cynic.* 1929. Reprint, Louisville: Westminster/John Knox, 1980.

Norén, Carol M. *The Woman in the Pulpit.* Nashville: Abingdon, 1991.

O'Brien, Conor Cruise. *On the Eve of the Millennium: The Future of Democracy through an Age of Unreason.* New York: Free Press, 1994.

O'Connor, Flannery. *Three by Flannery O'Connor.* New York: Signet, n.d.

Ong, Walter J., S.J. *Fighting for Life: Contest, Sexuality, and Consciousness.* Ithaca, N.Y.: Cornell University Press, 1981.

Oswald, Roy M. *Finding Leaders for Tomorrow's Churches: The Growing Crisis in Clergy Recruitment.* N.p.: Alban Institute, 1993.

Peterson, Eugene H. *Under the Unpredictable Plant: An Exploration in Vocational Holiness.* Grand Rapids: Eerdmans, 1992.

Placher, William C. *Narratives of a Vulnerable God: Christ, Theology, and Scripture.* Louisville: Westminster/John Knox, 1994.

Ramsey, Paul. *Basic Christian Ethics.* New York: Scribner's, 1950.

Resner, André, Jr. *Preacher and Cross: Reason and Message in Theology and Rhetoric.* Grand Rapids: Eerdmans, 1999.

Rich, Adrienne. *What Is Found There: Notebooks on Poetry and Politics.* New York: Norton, 1993.

Saunders, Stanley P., and Charles L. Campbell. *The Word on the Street: Performing the Scriptures in the Urban Context.* Grand Rapids: Eerdmans, 2000.

Schreiter, Robert J., C.P.P.S. *Reconciliation: Mission and Ministry in a Changing Social Order.* Maryknoll: N.Y.: Orbis, 1992.

Sittler, Joseph. *The Anguish of Preaching.* Philadelphia: Fortress, 1966.

―――. *The Ecology of Faith.* Philadelphia: Fortress, 1961.

Smalley, Beryl. *The Study of the Bible in the Middle Ages.* Oxford: Clarendon, 1941.

Snow, John H. *The Impossible Vocation: Ministry in the Mean Time.* Cambridge, Mass.: Cowley, 1988.

Spillers, Hortense J. *Black, White, and in Color: Essays on American Literature and Culture.* Chicago: University of Chicago Press, 2003.

Steinmetz, David C. "The Superiority of Pre-Critical Exegesis." In *The Theological Interpretation of Scripture,* edited by Stephen E. Fowl. Oxford: Blackwell, 1997.

Storey, Peter. "A Different Kind of Justice: Truth and Reconciliation in South Africa." *The Christian Century* 114, no. 25 (Sept. 10-17, 1997): 788-93.

Tannehill, Robert C. *The Sword of His Mouth.* Philadelphia: Fortress, 1975.

Tannen, Deborah. *The Argument Culture: Moving from Debate to Dialogue.* New York: Random House, 1998.

Taylor, Barbara Brown. *Home by Another Way.* Cambridge, Mass.: Cowley, 1999.

———. *When God Is Silent.* Cambridge, Mass.: Cowley, 1998.

Tillich, Paul. *The Shaking of the Foundations.* New York: Scribner's, 1948.

Truth and Reconciliation Commission of South Africa. *Report.* Vol. 1. Capetown: Juta, 1998.

Tufte, Edward R. *The Cognitive Style of PowerPoint.* Cheshire, Conn.: Graphics, 2003.

Volf, Miroslav. *Exclusion and Embrace: A Theological Exploration of Identity, Otherness, and Reconciliation.* Nashville: Abingdon, 1996.

Warren, Michael. *Seeing through the Media: A Religious View of Communication and Cultural Analysis.* Harrisburg, Pa.: Trinity Press International, 1992.

Wells, David F. *God in the Wasteland: The Reality of Truth in a World of Fading Dreams.* Grand Rapids: Eerdmans, 1994.

Wilder, Amos N. *Early Christian Rhetoric: The Language of the Gospel.* Cambridge, Mass.: Harvard University Press, 1964.

Wilken, Robert Louis. "In Defense of Allegory." In *Theology and Scriptural Imagination,* edited by L. Gregory Jones and James J. Buckley. Oxford: Blackwell, 1998.

Williams, Rowan. *A Ray of Darkness.* Cambridge, Mass.: Cowley, 1995.

Willimon, William. *Peculiar Speech.* Grand Rapids: Eerdmans, 1992.

Wuthnow, Robert. *After Heaven: Spirituality in America Since the 1950s.* Berkeley: University of California Press, 1998.

Yoder, John Howard. *Body Politics: Five Practices of the Christian Community before the Watching World.* Nashville: Discipleship Resources, 1992.

Index

About the Author

Richard Lischer is James T. and Alice Mead Cleland Professor of Preaching at Duke Divinity School. Before joining the Duke faculty, he served as pastor of Lutheran congregations in Illinois and Virginia. A graduate of Concordia Senior College and Concordia Seminary, he also holds an M.A. in English from Washington University in St. Louis and a Ph.D. in theology from the University of London. He is the author of numerous books on preaching, theology, and ministry, including *A Theology of Preaching: The Dynamics of the Gospel* and the prize-winning *The Preacher King: Martin Luther King, Jr. and the Word That Moved America*. He is also the co-editor (with William Willimon) of the *Concise Encyclopedia of Preaching*. The story of his first pastorate, *Open Secrets: A Memoir of Faith and Discovery*, has been widely anthologized, and his most recent Eerdmans book, *The Company of Preachers*, was named Best Book in ministry in 2002 by *Christianity Today*. *The End of Words* is based on his Lyman Beecher Lectures in Preaching delivered at Yale Divinity School. Professor Lischer and his wife live in Orange County, North Carolina.